SPELL
Albu~~x~~querque

Memoir of a "Difficult" Student

SPELL
Albu~~x~~querque

Memoir of a "Difficult" Student

TENNESSEE REED

CounterPunch
PETROLIA

AK PRESS

First published by
CounterPunch and AK Press 2009
© *CounterPunch* 2009
All rights reserved

CounterPunch
PO Box 228, Petrolia, California 95558

AK Press
674-A 23rd St, Oakland, California 94612-1163

ISBN 978-1904859888

A catalog record for this book is available from the Library of Congress

Library of Congress Control Number: 2008927317

Typeset in Minion Pro, designed by Robert Slimbach for Adobe Systems Inc.;
and Amplitude, designed by Christian Schwartz for The Font Bureau, Inc.

Printed and bound in Canada.

Design and typography by Tiffany Wardle de Sousa.

This book is dedicated to the teachers, principals, advisors and therapists who believed in me: Amy Faltz, JoAnne Hughes, Edythe Boone, Russ Henry, Dr. Beverly Smith-Miller, Dr. Barbara Penny-James, Dr. Susan McGee, Dr. John Ilita-White, Jenny Ruckleshaus, Professor Eleanor Dickinson, Professor Leon Litwack, Professor Barbara Christian, Professor Kathy Moran, Professor Elmaz Abinader, Professor Cynthia Scheinberg, and Professor Stephen Ratcliffe.

This book is in memory of Carrie Rozelle, founder of National Center of Learning Disabilities, friends Reginald Lockett, Nancy Hicks Maynard, David Perez, Daniel Patrick Cassidy, Elizabeth "Sister" Hope and Andrew Hope III, South African legend Miriam Makeba, and neighbor Mrs. Morine McClure.

Contents

Acknowledgments . . . . **ix**

Introduction by C. Paolo Caruso . . . . **xi**

Chapter 1: What My Disabilities Are And How They
Affect My Professional And Social Life **1**

Chapter 2: The Preschool Years **5**

Chapter 3: Kindergarten Through Third Grade **17**

Chapter 4: Fourth Through Sixth Grade **33**

Chapter 5: Seventh Through Ninth Grade **53**

Chapter 6: Tenth Through Twelfth Grade **83**

Chapter 7: California College of Arts and Crafts **97**

Chapter 8: Laney College **101**

Chapter 9: U.C. Berkeley **115**

Chapter 10: My Senior Year in College **135**

Chapter 11: My Graduation from College **151**

Chapter 12: Graduate School and My 3.55 GPA **153**

Chapter 13: My Campaign for Oakland School Board, District One. **169**

Timeline by Carla Blank **185**

Bibliography by Carla Blank **201**

Acknowledgments

My great thanks to Jeffrey St. Clair who first believed in this work and found a way to publish it through AK Press and Counterpunch.

Thank you to Cecilia Caruso for writing the Foreword, Carla Blank for writing the timeline, and Ishmael Reed for writing the publicity description.

Thank you to all of the people at CounterPunch and AK Press who worked on this project: Tiffany Wardle de Sousa for the excellent design, and Kjerstin Johnson, Kimberly Wilson-St. Clair, Alexander Cockburn and Alevtina Rae for the tireless copy-editing. Thank you to Ally Day and Kate Khatib for helping publicize the book, starting with my appearances at East Boston High School and Lesley University on October 2, 2008.

Great thanks to my wonderful friends: Jeni Romero, Elisa Miranda, Rosa and Ajani Cruz, Edythe Boone, Elaine and Jahn Overstreet, Lucia and Pablo Dominguez, Boadiba, Kathryn Takara, Karla Brundage, Natasha Harrington, Subira Shaw, Cecilia Caruso, Heather Nakasone, Eva Heinstein and Jody Roberts for answering my questions and for their continuing support.

Thank you to my mother, father, aunts, uncles, cousins, grandmothers, sister and brother-in-law for their kind words and support.

Introduction

By C. Paolo Caruso

I FIRST MET TENNESSEE REED IN 1991, WHEN SHE WAS A NINTH-GRADE student at New Age Academy in Berkeley, California. I was a second-year graduate student in the Law School (Boalt Hall) at the University of California, Berkeley and had decided to do some tutoring in order to make some extra money. I circulated posters around the campus and surrounding neighborhoods. Then, one day, I received a call from Tennessee's mother, Carla, who had seen one of my posters. She arranged for an interview and an introduction between Tennessee and me. We liked each other from the very beginning and it was agreed I would begin tutoring Tennessee immediately.

At that time, Tennessee was a strong C+ student, not failing anything, but not distinguishing herself either. Since this was Tennessee's last year at the Academy and she would be entering high school the following year, her parents were anxious for her to get into a good high school. It was imperative for her to improve her grades. We immediately set to work, focusing on English and Math.

I found Tennessee to be a very committed and receptive student. Working with her one-on-one, I was able to get results from that teenager that her teachers had simply been unable to achieve. We worked long and hard, time permitting, between my commitments at the law school. Tennessee became a passionate challenge for me.

Despite many hours of laughter, when I would sometimes have to put my foot down and remind her what was at stake, Tennessee became just as anxious as I was to prove what she was made of. And so she did. At the end of her ninth-grade year, Tennessee won nearly every award for academic excellence. Not only did she achieve the highest grades for that year, she achieved the highest grades in the history of the school! At her graduation, she was the undeniable "Queen for a day!" As her name was called for one award after another, her pride and belief in herself soared commensurately. When I saw her later that day, she was grinning from ear to ear. She was so happy and so pleased with herself.

I believe that ninth grade success was the turning point for a young lady who previously had not thought much of herself. The realization that she can do great things despite chronic health problems has served to sustain her over the years. In fact her belief in herself and drive to succeed have helped her do things many healthier people could not do. She has earned her bachelor's and master's degrees, published many books of poetry, developed skills in photography, ran for the school board in Oakland, edited others' writings, and taught school, among other accomplishments. And all the while, as she was succeeding at these phenomenal undertakings, she has never been free from constant back pain, neuropathy, learning disabilities or ADHD. Along the way, she has also had a bout of skin cancer and is now suffering from chronic pain.

I have always admired and cared deeply for Tennessee. We developed a bond those many years ago, which has lasted until today. I am honored to have been asked to write this introduction to *Spell Albuquerque*.

C. Paolo Caruso
April 4, 2008

CHAPTER ONE

What My Disabilities Are and How They Affect My Professional and Social Life

"Society's disability: One way of thinking, being and living is the right way and the only way of thinking, being and living."
— Tennessee Reed, May 21, 2002

BETWEEN EIGHTEEN MONTHS AND TWO YEARS OF AGE, I WAS diagnosed as having a speech and language-based communication disorder. I was late in expressing myself through language and slow in processing language. Unlike a normal child's speech pattern I would say a word and then not repeat it for six months. I was diagnosed as aphasic, which creates a speech pattern common to stroke and head trauma victims. I had my own language for a few years until I learned to speak English.

Aphasia affected my reading comprehension. My reading comprehension is a lot better than it used to be, thanks to my compensation skills. I can read most things once and understand them. This problem improved somewhere in my early twenties. I still prefer audio books. I can hear them, so therefore I can comprehend them better. I wish they had this technology when I was a child, although I did use read-along records. Now I can put audio books on my iPod Nano. In addition, I have trouble following spoken or written directions, especially multiple step directions. That hasn't improved much.

I have trouble with 3-dimensional perception, which affects drawing and measuring geometric shapes. I also have trouble with logical reasoning and solving equations. My problem with math equations has not improved. Even when I had a tutor and I studied the material rigorously, my math test results showed no improvement. If find even basic math difficult. Word problems, decimals and percentages are hard for me.

When I am shopping and there is a sale, it is hard for me to figure out what 10 per cent or 20 per cent off of the regular price is. Sometimes I have to ask someone what the sale price is. Algebra, geometry, trigonometry, calculus and statistics are disciplines where my disability hits the hardest. My math disability is called dyscalculia. It is like dyslexia.

I also have trouble with tasks that require small muscle control or hand-eye coordination, which means I have difficulty with cutting and folding, but that is improving a bit. I don't hold my writing or eating utensils in the proper way. I even have a hard time buttoning my blouses with small buttons. This is why I buy dressy tee shirts or tunics instead of blouses.

I was not diagnosed with Attention Deficit Hyperactivity Disorder until 1998 when I was tested at the University of California, Berkeley. When I was a small child, I was hyper. I took a lot of antibiotics and cough syrup for ear infections and colds. This caused hyperactivity because the ingredients included red and purple food dye. That's how I learned I had to cut food dye out of my diet. I also get rid of excess energy by swimming and doing low impact aerobics. I still talk too much sometimes and giggle inappropriately. Just like with the language-based disorder, it can flare up when I'm nervous, hungry, tired, sick, on my menstrual cycle and using the potent painkillers I now need to take everyday.

The ADHD has improved as well, but I still have a long way to go. I also don't take antibiotics anymore when I have an earache. My parents have never pushed me to take medicine to reduce ADHD behaviors and neither have my doctors or my teachers. While I was a member of AmeriCorps, some of my colleagues and bosses strongly suggested that I take anti-ADHD medications. AmeriCorps was established in 1993 by former President Bill Clinton. It is a network of more than 3,000 non-profit organizations, public agencies, and faith-based organizations. Mission statement: to serve to create safe, clean, and healthy neighborhood environments through education, collaboration and action; to instill high levels of individual and neighborhood responsibility teaching children and youth healthy environmental practices that lead to an increase in food security, ecologically healthier urban watersheds, a decrease in solid waste, and an increase in academic skills through service learning.

When I was a young girl, I was told that I had autistic-like behaviors because I have an abnormal way of socializing. This was a theory. There was no diagnosis. I feel that my social anxiety is mostly related to the disabilities. Learning-disabled people tend to have difficulty picking up cues and following social etiquette. For me, emotional baggage and chronic pain are part of the package as well. According to my pre-school teacher, I didn't play with the other children that often. At that age I had frequent ear infections. I was in constant pain. Now, at age thirty-one, I have chronic back pain, sciatica and small-fiber polyneuropathy, a very painful condition that is caused by a mild degeneration of the small nerve endings. This is why I am taking pain medications. As a student, I had to pay attention to my academic life more than my social life so I could be up to par with the rest of the class, and that took up most of my time. A lot of people don't understand why I have trouble socializing even if they have known me all of my life.

Because I have disabilities, people make a lot of negative assumptions about me, whether they are teachers, bosses, classmates, co-workers, family and even friends. The most common assumptions are that I am lazy, that I'm not bright, that I am trying to get out of something, that I'm not interested in a subject, or that I am selfish. I have gotten used to these assumptions. I used to think these assumptions were personal to me. At age thirty-one I know they were not personal to me. Assumptions are based on ignorance. This is not anyone's fault. It is what it is. Even though I know the assumptions are not personal to me, this doesn't make them less frustrating. Now that I am an adult, I have a choice not to be around these people.

No one knows what caused my learning disability, and no one will ever know. It could have been the overdose of the childhood vaccinations I took at the age of three or four months that made me sick. According to my uncle, Dr. Michael LeNoir, a pediatric allergist based in Oakland, California, children should only get three vaccinations at a time. I had six at one time, which overloaded my immune system, causing me to get very sick. The disabilities could also be a result of the birth trauma I suffered when the umbilical cord wrapped around my neck cutting off oxygen. The chronic ear infections showed up at the time most children begin to pick up language. Learning disabilities, ADHD and physical disabilities exist on both sides of my family. My disability is neither serious nor mild. This causes frustration for family, friends, teachers, classmates, bosses, colleagues and myself. Even I don't fully understand my disabilities even though I have lived with them all of my life.

In schooling I did well with teachers who were older and had years of experience in teaching. I didn't do so well with young teachers or teachers who barely had any experience. Sometimes I had teachers who didn't go to school to get the necessary training to become teachers. In college I got nervous when it came time to give my professors my accommodation letters because I didn't know how they would react. Accommodation letters, a standard practice that is suggested for students with disabilities, inform their teachers in a way that provides some privacy about their particular needs and suggested accommodations. Some of them looked at these requests not knowing what to think. They would put the letters in their briefcases and I never heard from them again. Others responded with frustration and anger. Some did all they could to make sure I got my accommodations.

CHAPTER TWO

The Preschool Years

AFTER MY DIAGNOSIS, THE NEXT PROBLEM WAS SCHOOLING, because it was recommended that I start school at two years of age in order to improve my social skills and to help my speech. Between age eight months and two, I had gone to childcare where other children were sometimes present so my mom, Carla Blank, could start working on "The Children's Troupe," a non-profit performing arts program begun by her and Jody Roberts. I was eight months old when I started daycare. The woman who took care of me was named Ms. Rowe, whom I considered my adopted grandmother. When I was five and six she was my Brownie leader also. Mom wanted me to stay with her. Unfortunately, her husband Ned was sick, so she recommended my going to another caretaker's house. I don't remember the woman's name. She was from Peru, a mother herself, and probably was in her late twenties or early thirties.

The caretaker lived down the street from Ms. Rowe and took care of six other children. Instead of beginning to learn positive social skills, I began to learn prejudice, anger, frustration, hurt, embarrassment, jealousy, isolation and shame because she shamed me in front of the other children for still wearing diapers and drinking out of a bottle at age two. She used to let me sleep longer because she didn't want to deal with changing my diapers or feeding me a bottle. Once my mother realized this, she took me out of her care.

Longfellow Day Nursery School was my first real school. It was a half-day program in the Berkeley Public Schools. I don't remember anything about it. All I remember was being potty trained, which was required in order for me to attend Longfellow. It was required by law that I work with a speech therapist. I found out later my therapist was the friend of writer Cecil Brown. Her name was Ms. Rucker and she was from Norway.

In the afternoon, I went to my good friend Beverly Smith-Miller's house and hung out with her sons, Jimmy and Troy, and some other children. I only stayed at Longfellow School for one year. I then transferred to Children's Community Center (CCC), an A.M. cooperative nursery school where the parents volunteered once a week, because Mom really liked the afternoon daycare workers Ms. Boone and Mr. Henry. I am friends with Ms. Boone to this day.

During the summers of 1980 and 1981, we lived in New Hampshire because my dad, Ishmael Reed, was invited to lecture at Dartmouth College. While we lived in New Hampshire we traveled to New York City, New York State, Massachusetts, Vermont, Maine and New Jersey, to see friends and relatives, and also to go on sight-seeing day trips.

In 1981, I started at the same daycare in the church that I went to in 1980, but I wasn't there for long because they decided to have me transfer daycares for not being able to stand in line. The daycare teacher suggested that I go to a daycare across the border in Norwich, Vermont. Norwich was just across the border from Hanover and it was actually in closer proximity to our house than the old daycare was. I don't remember the house, but I do remember the daycare in bits and pieces, which worked out fine.

Speaking of traveling, I travel a lot. When I was five months old, I took my first flight to Japan with my mother for a month-long trip. We went to Tokyo, Kyoto and Osaka because my mother was touring with her dance collaborator Suzushi Hanayagi in a series of performances. I went to Japan in 1996 again to these three cities and other cities as well, accompanying Mom and Dad. Dad was there in connection with the publication of his novel, *Japanese by Spring*.

With the exception of Delaware and Rhode Island, I have visited every Northeastern and Mid-Atlantic state. I passed through Delaware and Rhode Island traveling on the Northeast Regional Amtrak line that runs between Washington, D.C. and Boston. I have visited Virginia, Kentucky, Tennessee and Florida in the Southeast. Illinois is the only state I have visited in the Midwest, and Oregon and Washington are the only states I have visited in the Northwest. In the Southwest I have traveled to Nevada, Arizona and New Mexico.

I have also visited Alaska, Hawaii, Martinique, England, the Netherlands and Germany. I saw a little bit of France when we exited the Basel Airport to drive up to Frieburg, Germany. I saw a bit of Switzerland for a few hours. I traveled to Niagara Falls, Canada for a few hours when visiting Buffalo, and to Tijuana and Ensenada in Mexico for a few hours when visiting San Diego. I would like to see more of the United States, the Caribbean, Europe and Asia. I would also love to see Nigeria, Ghana, Zimbabwe, South Africa, Brazil and Peru. I have been to most of the major U.S. airports, and I have frequent flyer miles on American, Delta, United, Northwest and jetBlue. I have also traveled on TWA, ATA, Southwest, National, Aloha, Alaska, Continental, USAirways, British Airways, Air France, Swissair, Lufthansa, JAL, Japan Air System and ANA. I wrote a poem about an American Airlines commercial that came out in 1995 or 1996. American Airlines has a lot of significance to me because it was my first airline and I have flown on it the most. I have also been to many museums all over the world, which is where the paintings come in.

STUDY OF A YOUNG SMILING FLIGHT ATTENDANT

In an American Airlines ad
that appears on CNN
a young stewardess
walks down the gateway
With a curious frown
she's looking at airplanes
parked at the gates
She is like the woman
in *Portrait of Victorine Meurent*
by the painter Edouard Manet

The plane takes off
It's a DC-10
Segue to inside the cabin
A little girl kneels in her mom's lap
held close and tight
as she looks over the back of a seat
The mother and daughter are right out of
Madonna of the Chair by Raphael
Her mother is pointing at something

as they sit and talk
by the window

The young stewardess appears again
smiling at all the passengers
like the woman in Pontormo's
Portrait of a Young Woman

Segue to inside in a heavenly blue sky
The American Airlines plane is flying
like the angel in *A Maiden's Dream*
by Bernadino Luini

The screen turns black
Ad copies roll in white
as a piano continues to play
the advertising jingle

I wish I'd meet this stewardess
with her inviting smile
who fooled me into thinking
I would find her in real life

I found her in a movie
called *Baby's Day Out*
She played a mother
looking for her baby
who had memorized the images
in a book
and traveled
all over town
looking for the images
just like I traveled
over four centuries
to find images
in the world's museums
that matched
that perfect world

I came back to CCC in the fall of 1980. One of the morning program teachers told my parents that I "didn't draw my age." She refused to put my artwork on the wall. Now, art experts consider my paintings as "Outsider Art." This teacher just didn't like the way I drew. My mom didn't believe in this young teacher's way of thinking, so she had the drawings made into dinner plates. My mother gave me coloring books and pens. Both of my parents are artists. My father is a writer, retired UC Berkeley professor emeritus, publisher, editor and jazz pianist. My mother is a writer, editor, choreographer, dramatic artist, director, and jazz violinist. I am a writer, editor, web designer, administrative assistant and photographer. I drew a lot throughout my life until I developed neuropathy. Now I do digital photography, which I make into greeting cards and email to family and friends.

Often an IEP (Individualized Education Program) evaluator from the school district would test me at school. I don't remember this incident, but a young woman who was testing me took me into a dark broom closet. She ridiculed me for my reactions, which were anxiety and fear. I think there would have been something wrong with me if I didn't react that way. I remember that closet with detail. It was narrow, quite dark and hot. There was some old white paint on it. After that, I wouldn't go anywhere near it. I really liked the room where the closet was located, though.

I had a few good friends at CCC. Their names were Hillel, Shira and Yolanka. Hillel had a baby sister, Eva, born in 1984, when we both were seven. I remember going to the Martin Luther King Junior High School pool with Hillel a few times and hanging out at his apartment in Berkeley. I also remember helping his family move to their home in 1988. Eva and I are still friends. She lives in Cambridge, Massachusetts where she is getting her doctorate and teaching. Eva is twenty-four years old. I saw her this past October when I read at Lesley University. Hillel is thirty-one and lives in Toronto with his fiancé getting his Master's Degree.

Laughing, Shira and I used to run around the climbing structure at Children's Community Center. She and I swam at the Martin Luther King Junior High School pool in Berkeley as well. At her home I remember an overnight birthday party when she turned seven. I also remember her cat Rapunsel, and her dad, Jules, shoving two wasps off of the kitchen window with a broom. Shira's boyfriend studied at Mills College at the same time as me. I spoke with Shira after graduation. She and her boyfriend moved to Los Angeles shortly after that and I haven't heard from them since.

Yolanka had a Czech mother and an American father from Chicago. She had quite a few siblings, but I only remember an infant brother. I remember going with them to the Co-op (now Andronico's) on Shattuck and Cedar because they lived right down the street. I haven't heard from Yolanka, either. My mom ran into her dad in 1995 when Yolanka was a freshman at Temple University. Yolanka's dad was the music teacher at CCC. We often sang "Surrey with the Fringe on Top" from *Oklahoma!*

In the fall of 1981, after my second trip to New Hampshire, I took my first BART ride and went to Cordonices Park. I remember I couldn't nap for a lot of reasons, including excess energy from the medications, stress, overstimulation and illness. I remember giving one of the daycare teachers an attitude for telling me I couldn't go outside because I didn't nap. I turned my back to her and played with the doll house as a way to shut her out, which is something I do when I am angry even to this day. Turning my back to people. She was a child herself, literally, because she was in her late teens or early twenties. I still remember her angry demeanor and her telling me that I couldn't go outside.

I got punished often during my early school years. This damaged my self-esteem because I would be ridiculed in front of the class, and since I couldn't process information well, I didn't understand why I was being punished. Most of the time I didn't do anything bad enough to cause such a reaction. The teachers didn't have the skills to work with my learning and social problems. They were acting out of fear and frustration. Their emotions came out in anger. The teachers usually ridiculed and humiliated the disabled kids, the poor kids, the black kids, and the Latino kids. They barely ridiculed the rich white kids and Asian kids, even if what they did was much worse. Their punishment was over the top.

From age three up to age eight I went to two therapists, named Dr. Hughes and Dr. Faltz. I had hearing tests there as well as at Kaiser Hospital. They helped improve my speech and they encouraged me to write. At school, when I drew pictures, I would tell stories to practice.

My classmates at school would ask me, "Why are you talking when you draw pictures?"

When I was five, I lived in Alaska for a month and a half when Dad participated in a conference at the Sitka Community Center. I didn't have to go to daycare. This made things less stressful for me. Mom taught dance to middle school children at Sitka National Historical Park. I don't really remember the kids except for hanging out with the late Andrew Hope's six-year-old twin granddaughters. I don't remember their names, but I remember how nice they were to me. We used to take walks in the forest to the lake where I would take off my red saltwater sandals and wade in the water while Mom taught. I went out on a fishing boat with two Native American friends and I caught a rock cod. I remember that. We were visiting Andy and the late Elizabeth Sister Hope. Sister was an Inuit and Andy a Tlingit. Sister died of colon cancer in October of 1997. I feel that she got colon cancer because the fish up in the Arctic Circle where she grew up were probably contaminated. I don't remember Sister that much nor do I really remember anything about that trip. I vaguely remember the house, just the kitchen. Andy and Sister's son, Ishmael Hope, named after my father, who is my godbrother, had a little girl in December of 2007 named Elizabeth. Ishmael was seven or eight months old the summer we were up there. I haven't seen him in ten years, and I don't really have an interaction with him. He is a writer of post-modern fiction and plays. In 1998, my parents were made Tlingit clan members during an all-day potluck ceremony in Sitka. My father was required to do a Halibut dance as part of the ceremony.

This was the summer when I started learning how to swim. Mom chose the Martin Luther King Junior High School pool in Berkeley for my lessons. I have also swam at Willard Junior High School in Berkeley, the El Cerrito Swim Center, Strawberry Canyon in Berkeley, the Spieker Aquatics Complex in Berkeley, Golden Bear in Berkeley, the Trefethen Aquatics Center at Mills College, the Claremont Hotel in Oakland, the downtown Berkeley YMCA, the Jewish Community Center in Pittsburgh,

Pennsylvania, the Diplomat in Piedmont, New York, Harvard University and the University of Washington, Seattle.

When I travel, I also like to swim. I've swam in hotel swimming pools in Albuquerque, New Mexico; Las Vegas, Nevada; Pearl River, New York; Nagoya, Japan; Asilomar, Disneyland, San Diego, Santa Monica and Universal City in California; Honolulu, Hawaii; New York City; Louisville, Kentucky and a small town on the island of Martinique. I really liked the pools at the Millennium U.N. Plaza Hotel in New York and at the Mandalay Bay in Las Vegas. I also liked the pool on the roof of the Gault Hotel in Louisville where I could view the Ohio River while swimming. I was there assisting Dad with his book, *Bigger Than Boxing*, about Muhammad Ali.

I have also swam in the Pacific off of California, Hawaii and Washington, the Atlantic off of Massachusetts and Florida and the Caribbean Sea off of Martinique; the Russian River in Guerneville, California; Lake Anza in Berkeley; Green Lake in Seattle, Washington; and Lake Temescal in Oakland. I swam on the Berkeley Barracudas team during the summer of 1992, which was the closest to competition swimming I ever got. That was again at MLK. I swim three days a week at the Downtown Berkeley YMCA.

In the spring of 2005, when I was in graduate school, I took a fitness swim class in Mills College's pool. I had an excellent swim coach at Mills. He was in his early thirties, and he was a professional swim coach. I realized that I still swam like a child because it had been years since I took lessons. He helped me improve my kicking, my crawl, my backstroke (which is still difficult) and my breaststroke. He helped me begin my butterfly stroke. A coach at the YMCA helped me improve the butterfly, and another coach at the YMCA taught me how to flip-turn. Unfortunately, I can't do breast stroke and butterfly anymore due to a spine-related condition.

I did Brownies for two years and from age five through age eight I either went to the Brownie House or Ms. Rowe's house after school. Ms. Rowe's Brownie name was "Opossum." I also was a part of the Brownies when I was five. We had our camp at the Berkeley Marina at Adventure

Playground. The Brownie headquarters was at a home in Berkeley. It was a brown shingled house on Rose Street, and the front room had a painted brownie sitting on a mushroom and in the back room were painted oceans and a lighthouse. I made up stories about this that were incorporated into poems. Mrs. Rowe taught me how to fold socks, how to tie my shoes and how to sew. I made some Christmas tree ornaments. She also helped me with my homework. The Brownie House is no longer in existence. It is now a residence. I pass it quite often.

At age five, I began to start writing poetry and I also learned how to dance. My first poems were inspired by my mother's company, The Children's Troupe of Roberts and Blank, that she and her long time friend, Jody Roberts had founded. She and Jody met at Mills College in Oakland where they attended graduate school in the dance department. Mom was thirty and Jody was twenty-seven with a one and a half year old son. Their ideas for The Children's Troupe started in October of 1977 when I was eight months old. Their book *Live on Stage!*, published in 1995 is about their teaching techniques and performance scripts. It was adopted by the states of North Carolina, Tennessee, Mississippi, and Idaho. This is where I began to associate with Jody's daughter, Taya, and her friends, Tara, Molly, Julie, Portia, Rebecca, Selina and Regina.

I was only four, but my first memory of rehearsals was when Rebecca wore white stirrup tights and a blue lacy tunic with a gold-shimmer bird mask while she danced in a production of *Firebird* composed by Igor Stravinsky. She reminded me of one of the cranes I saw at the Berkeley Marina. She was tall, gorgeous and slender. Rebecca and I were very good friends. She stayed with me over the years while my parents took trips. She also was one of my babysitters and birthday party helpers. I remember going to a relative's birthday party in Tilden Park in the summer of 1993 and playing catch with Rebecca's brother, Morgan, and his friend. We took her cousin, Jane, who was then five, to the carousel and the pony rides. After that we went to her parents' home in Albany, a town just north of Berkeley, off of Solano Avenue, where we had ice cream and cake. Rebecca, Jane and I took the dog Josie for a walk around the neighborhood.

Rebecca made me laugh a lot. One evening we were watching *White Men Can't Jump* on TV and I kept looking at her to see what her reaction to it was. She kept saying, "Stop staring at me, Tennessee!" But she was laughing, too. That was in the fall of 1993. We also saw *Meet the Parents* with Ben Stiller when it came into the theaters during the fall of 2000. We laughed throughout the movie. I saw Rebecca at Berkeley Bowl Marketplace in September of 2008. She is a daycare worker in Berkeley.

Regina was the princess in the production *The Starcleaner Reunion*, composed by Randy Craig. It was based on a book by Cooper Edens, which I still read to children when they come over. Regina wore a long, flowing, bright pink dress, had a sparkly tiara and pink shoes. She had sparkles on her face. She reminds me of the Disney princesses. I remember watching the dress rehearsals at the People's Theatre at Fort Mason in San Francisco and being awed by her costume. I couldn't keep my eyes off of her. One of the poems I wrote when I was five was in honor of her. It was called "A Fairy's House In Your Life" and was published in my first poetry collection, *Circus in the Sky: Poems 1982–1988*.

Regina spent the night at our house many times. I remember us laying on the sofa bed and laughing when I was about six or seven. She was a very sweet person. She was patient when I asked her questions about her sprained ankle. I haven't seen her since 1996 when she came out to visit family and friends from Yale University in New Haven, Connecticut, where she was studying to become a midwife. She now lives in Albuquerque where she works as a midwife. She has two sons. She has lived there since 1997 or 1998.

Portia also babysat me. She would frequently take me to the Martin Luther King Junior High pool for the public swim. She spent about ten days with me when my parents went to Italy in April of 1990. I was in seventh grade. Portia had a great laugh. She used to ride home in the car with us on Monday, Wednesday and Friday after The Children's Troupe's session was over. She lived at the bottom of Rose Street in Berkeley. One day she had been crying by the time Mom picked me up from Children's Community Center. I was about four or five and I remember being concerned about her crying. I asked her what had happened but she didn't really give me an answer. She kept smiling, probably because she saw how worried I was. I never got the answer to why she was crying.

From 1998–2000, Portia was an assistant to my acupuncturist, Dr. Robert Johns. I would come there to be treated for earaches and to help my mouth heal after wisdom teeth surgery. The last time I saw her she was carrying her first daughter. She got married in May of 2000, but I didn't go to the wedding because I was over in England studying. She has two daughters, ages eight and five. She lives about an hour northeast of Oakland in a town called Hercules.

Now these former Children's Troupe students are in their thirties or forties. Most of them went to get degrees in medicine, law and education. Some became artists. Selina won an award at Sundance for producing a film. I don't remember what it was called.

I also spent a lot of time with these young women because they babysat me and were in the Brownies with me. I hung out with Taya during the summer months because I spent a lot of time at Jody's. I had known her since I was three days old. Taya gave me my first pair of Guess jeans the summer I was going to fifth grade and she was going to ninth grade. I wore the jeans on the trip I took to Arizona in May of 1991 when I was in eighth grade and on stage with Tehiya Camp, a Jewish day camp in El Cerrito, where I performed a "Cat in the Hat" rhyme with another ten-year-old girl, during the summer of 1987.

I remember Taya putting some brown eye shadow on me when I was eight. She was about twelve. I remember all of the animals they had: two dogs named Tasha and Rosy, three cats named Shadow, Socks and Kitty, a bird named Chicory, a rabbit named Chim-Chim and a rat named Ratso. Taya has just returned to the Bay Area after attending college and medical school in Southern California and then moving to New York City for a three-year residency. Taya got married in 2003 and is the mother of a very young infant.

My father, a world-renowned author, influenced me to write and my mom inspired me to dance. Dad began to write in his teens and his first book, *Freelance Pallbearers,* was published when he was twenty-nine. He encountered some of the same problems in school as I, even more severe. He was beaten up by one teacher for being "smart." One teacher slapped him so hard that Grandma Reed withdrew him from school. The only teacher in grammar school who didn't judge him as a "discipline problem" was a black teacher, Hortense Nash, who recognized his talent.

My parents met in New York while performing a multimedia show called *Black*. Dad read poetry while Mom danced. The projected slides were created by Aldo Tambellini. Mom started dancing as a young child and she started teaching dance at the age of twelve. Both of my parents taught at the University of California, Berkeley and have traveled around the world doing workshops and poetry readings. That also explains why I travel so much. I have been invited to read in other places as well. I have traveled around the Bay Area and around the Southern, Western and Eastern States, Hawaii, Alaska, England, the Netherlands, Germany and Japan to read. My inspirations for writing came from Anne Frank, Langston Hughes, Jessica Hagedorn, Rudolfo Anaya and Kristin Hunter. The first poem I remember writing was called "Thursday's Rainbow." I was five years old when I wrote it. I got this idea from a thermos bottle I had that came with my lunch box. The thermos bottle had rainbows and clowns on it. That explains my fascination for clowns and rainbows. It was published in the *San Francisco Examiner*.

THURSDAY'S RAINBOW

One day when the rainbow was coming
the rain began to drizzle.
A person sat on a swing in the sky.
She was just perfect on the swing.
It was really drizzling.
It was a circus in the sky.
The rainbow was just perfectly there.
And the girl swang all around the world.
She was so high.
Higher than me.
She was really upside down in the sky.
She was so beautiful.
She was looking like a black person.
She looked inside sky.
And the rainbow was still there in the sky.
She had the beautiful colors in the sky.

CHAPTER THREE

Kindergarten Through Third Grade

I N THE FALL OF 1982, I STARTED KINDERGARTEN AT KAISER SCHOOL in Oakland. At that time kindergarten was only half time. I was in class from 9 AM to noon and then I went to CCC from 1 to 6 PM spending most of the time sleeping. Kindergarten was when feelings like anger, shame, embarrassment, isolation, jealousy, sadness and hopelessness became more and more every day feelings. I didn't know those words, but I knew what those feelings were. My mom observed Kaiser School when I was still at Children's Community Center. The city of Oakland did IEP assessment tests on me and decided my neighborhood school, Santa Fe Elementary School, was not the right fit for me. The teacher my mother observed in the spring, and who was excellent, caught mono in the fall when I entered kindergarten, and remained out for the rest of the year. A new teacher came in. She was quite young. I think she was the age that I am now, maybe even younger. She was frustrated at my inability to read at what for her was a normal age.

During a parent/teacher conference, this teacher told Mom that I would never be able to read or write. Mom told me recently that during the process of our learning to read, we had to cut words out and paste them on to a piece of paper. She assumed that because I had difficulty cutting that I wouldn't learn to read. What she didn't understand was that my speech and language disability was also connected to small motor skills like cutting, as opposed to large motor skills like walking. I learned to read, write, figure days of the week and how to tell time in six months at home thanks to Mom and Dad. I should have been learning this in school. When my teacher discovered my newly acquired reading and writing skills, she was shocked.

I first learned to read when Dad's friend, the late Ted Joans, author of *Funky Jazz Poems*, among many others, bought me a book and record of *The Three Billy Goats Gruff* at the Ashby BART flea market in Berkeley. Ted Joans was considered the greatest jazz poet of the twentieth century. Scholastic Records published the record in 1963. The storyteller was Bob Thomas, and Arthur Rubenstein composed the music. I also liked Walt Disney's version of *Peter and the Wolf*. Sterling Holloway, who sings some of the Disney songs I like, was the storyteller. The music was composed by Sergei Prokofiev, and the record was the soundtrack from the 1946 short movie of Disney's *Peter and the Wolf*. My mom, seeing my reaction to read-along records, bought me other read-along record books from Disney movies like *Peter Pan*, *Cinderella*, *Pinocchio*, *The Hobbit*, *Alice and Wonderland*, and *Mary Poppins*. I also had a compilation tape with a read-along book called *The Best of Disney: Volume II*, which I loved. When I babysat my cousin Lina recently, she really enjoyed looking at the images and listening to the music. I noticed that the images and music calmed her down when she had an upset stomach. She was trying to read the words on the page by following them with her finger. The songs put her to sleep, so for her first birthday I made her CDs with these songs and made a copy of the book. I still enjoy Disney recordings. I have found these songs online and now they are on my iPod.

In Kindergarten I was speaking short phrases. I learned language through songs and rhythm. I remember dancing to the music in class. I learned some things faster than others. I was slow in math and reading but I had learned the days of the week and how to tell time pretty fast. I don't really remember who my friends were in kindergarten or what my social skills were like. I was focusing so much on the rudiments of learning. Mom said that I was good friends with a young French-Vietnamese girl. I vaguely remember her. I do remember my hyperactivity from the medication I took for ear infections. They made me sleep-deprived and hyper, which affected my mood and performance in class. I vividly recall Mom questioning my doctor because he kept giving me the pills despite my reaction. Now Kaiser has a policy that antibiotics should not be used for earaches but in my case the antibiotics were needed because the infections might spread to my internal organs if they weren't treated.

The red eyes and high fever I got were warning signs. After doing some research on the complications of ear infections, I found that my symptoms were a warning sign that the infection could have spread to the bone, causing mastitis, or to the brain and spinal cord, causing spinal meningitis. When the nurses saw my red eyes, they took me in immediately instead of having me wait. I never cried. I suffered in silence. As a child, I became in-tune with my body. I noticed that my right nostril is defective. It gets stuffed up instead of running. The ear aches were always the right ear.

There are a few things I remember about kindergarten in terms of socialization. I remember watching the third- and fourth-grade girls playing jump rope singing, "Windy, windy, weather. We all jump in together: kindergarten, first grade, second grade, third grade, fourth grade, fifth grade, sixth grade," and whatever grade the kids were in they would hop in. The kids would also jump in when the girls said what month their birthdays were in. I remember Kaiser as being a racially diverse school.

My class sang a medley of Christmas songs right before school let out for our two-week holiday. We all stood on stage in rows with the tallest kids in the back and the shortest kids in the front. I don't remember the songs we sang, but I remember that being my first performance. The narrator was a skinny girl with long, blonde braids. She had on a white blouse, a blue corduroy jumper dress, red knee socks and white Mary Jane shoes. She wore knee socks a lot and always had to pull them up. She did that in front of the microphone on stage. We staged a puppet show of *The Wizard of Oz*. I was Dorothy. I memorized the lines. It took a few weeks. I also helped Mom make a *papier-mâché* puppet. The singing and the memorizing helped me with language just like in pre-school.

I left Kaiser School in the spring of 1983 because I was struggling. I was supposed to stay there through sixth grade. I remember Mom and me visiting the school I was going to transfer to, Park Day School, a private K-8 school, at its old site in Montclair. In the coming fall it was going to move to 43rd Street off of Telegraph Avenue in North Oakland. I got in on a scholarship. My treatment at Park School would scar my emotional development for many years.

I started K/1 at Park Day School in the fall of 1983. Mom first thought that I should be home-schooled but she wanted me to think of socializing as a positive part of my life. There was construction going on in the hallway outside of class, which made my panic attacks worse. I still get startled around loud noise. I hate construction noise, loud music at concerts and festivals, fireworks and thunder. I also hate darkness, tight spaces, crowds and noisy places. I don't like it when people sit too close to me, or when I am forced into a cramped environment. Now that I am in my thirties, I have the choice not to go to festivals or other places where my fears are tested. I don't go to the movies because the sound system is too loud. I don't like restaurants that much either because of the crowds and loud noises. I wait for the movies to come out on Direct TV and usually eat at home. I have begun to enjoy construction cranes, however. They don't make an awful sound and they look like very tall sculptures. To me they are pieces of art.

I didn't enjoy the K/1 school year. Because of my "behavioral problems," I was punished many times that year. I remember some of the incidents clearly. I remember one day I refused to clean up because I was mad at the teachers. The teachers were angry and because they were upset, I didn't get one of the lollipops that a boy was passing around the class. He'd just had a baby sister. It was pink lollipop that said, "It's a girl." The teachers made it clear that they were angry with me by telling the student that I wouldn't get a lollipop and why I wasn't going to get one. He didn't seem to care. He just moved on. I was angry, jealous and embarrassed.

Another time, both of the teachers were so frustrated with me they made me sit on the royal blue carpet while the class lined up for lunch. I don't remember what I did, but I remember my classmates staring at me. A friend of mine, Nili, wanted to help, but she didn't know what to do. I don't remember what they said to me or what happened after that. All I know is that I started to develop a prejudice toward older white women. I also taught myself to see mean-spirited and angry people as physically ugly. I built up anger toward authority figures and learned not to trust people until I really got to know them. I still hold these thoughts and feelings at the age of thirty-one. I have quit jobs and lost many friends because of these feelings.

I remember one day in school during my K/1 year when we were given a sheet of paper with planets and stars on them. I didn't understand the directions because there were so many, were said only once and went by incredibly fast. I started drawing inside the outlined stars and planets. About twenty minutes later, I looked over at a boy named Adam, the boy who had the baby sister, and I noticed him drawing a red spaceship. I remember feeling my heart sink to my stomach. My friend Chandrika pointed out that I was supposed to draw something on the blank part of the page and told on me to the teachers. Everyone in the class looked in my direction. I was so embarrassed. I was mad at Chandrika because of her big mouth.

My teachers shamed me in front of the class often. The class would turn and look at me. In order to justify this nasty behavior, they would say, "The reason your classmates are staring at you is because…" I wasn't the only one they did this to. At that age, a person can't help taking this kind of behavior personally, but twenty-five years later I realize that the anger was directed at me, even though they weren't really angry *with* me. Instead they were nervous and frustrated because they weren't trained to understand my learning process. I learned that anger is a mask of other feelings like frustration, fear, hurt and jealousy. The children didn't really care what was going on because they never reacted to the way others were being treated. Either that or they were uncomfortable. They were only five or six. There was some teasing, but a lot of the teasing I received didn't happen until fourth grade and beyond.

I had a hard two years because of one kid who had serious problems. Her name was Miranda R. She showed signs of having a mental illness or being prone to becoming mentally ill as an adult. Maybe she had severe ADHD, or severe depression, or severe emotional problems. To me, Miranda R was physically, emotionally and spiritually ugly because she was both verbally and physically abusive towards me. She often punched me in the stomach after school in sight of the teachers. They didn't do anything. They told me that I had provoked her. She and her friends one day surrounded me at lunchtime. I don't remember exactly how many girls were there, but I think there were about four or five of them. They started pulling down my navy blue sweat pants and giggling. Some of my friends took part. This is when I started to notice that sometimes my friends' behaviors had changed for the worse by friends of theirs.

It felt like the harassment went on for a long time. Luckily, I had on a green leotard, so my blue floral patterned underwear wasn't all the way exposed. It was just the panty line. Again, the teachers saw this and didn't do anything. They just stared. As I grew older I noticed the teachers would tell me to ignore such abuse, even if I was being verbally or physically assaulted by classmates, or they called me too sensitive, or they blamed me for why my classmates were treating me this way. School bullying has now become a national issue.

A few of my friends were good friends with Miranda R. Miranda R would sometimes be at my friends' birthday parties or sometimes she would be in the car with me when the parents would carpool us on field trips. Sometimes she would sit next to me. That was too close for comfort. The year I left Park School, she was expelled.

During this time of my life, I looked forward to birthday parties. I would invite my friends. My mom would buy delicious cakes at Neldon's Bakery and my friends gave me presents. We would go out in the back garden and play if the weather was good. My mom had helpers. They were her students: Portia, Rebecca, Jenny, and Regina. These parties lasted until I was eight.

I was also involved in dance and theater at Park School. I performed in *The Wizard of Oz*. I was the Good Witch of the South. I wore a red dress with gold or silver sequins, red tights and red plastic fisherman sandals. The second year I was there, I performed in *The Nutcracker*. I was the Arabian Dancer. "Arabian Coffee" is my favorite song from *The Nutcracker*. We performed at Oakland Technical High School. I wore a green long sleeve leotard and blue baggy pants. Doing drama and dance helped both my coordination and my language skills and through those classes I learned how to compensate by reading the lines over and over, memorizing the words, and expanding my vocabulary. That's why it is important for art and music to be taught in the schools. Some people don't think these classes are important but they raise students' math, reading and test scores. Art is also an important form of socialization.

Another thing I would look forward to was coming home and reading an article out of the newspaper. My dad would choose an article from the op-ed page of *The New York Times*, and I would read it and then explain it to him. He taught my older half-sister, Timothy, how to read and write the same way. When she came to the Bay Area from New York at the age of eleven to live with my parents, she had little education. She is quite smart. Herb Kohl, the educator, tested her and called her the fastest learner he had encountered. Kohl was instrumental in getting Timothy into a private school, where she made up for lost time. While a teenager, she wrote a novel that Anne Freegood at Random House wanted to publish. She didn't finish it because her mother demanded that she return to Brooklyn for the "summer." Instead of Timothy returning to school in California, she was kept in New York and didn't return to Oakland for two years. Timothy was diagnosed as schizophrenic at age twenty-eight. Her first novel, *Showing Out*, was published in 2003. The theater version, directed by Rome Neal, received a rave review in *The New York Sun*. Timothy is now writing a second novel, *Walking Through Brooklyn*.

One thing really I enjoyed between the ages of five and eight was the evening outings with writer and playwright Adrienne Kennedy, author of the breakthrough surrealist play, *The Funny House of the Negro*, and many others. Adrienne came out to Berkeley for three semesters over a three-year period to teach. Mom and Dad would go to events at Cal that weren't suitable for children, so I would stay with Adrienne most of that time in her apartment on campus at the Women's Faculty Club. I remember that the room had a window that faced the north side of campus with a large tree in front of it. The desk was right in front of the window. Adrienne's bed was to the left of the desk parked up against the wooden wall. I also remember the lobby. It had a long, wooden hallway with big, white chairs and sofas. A large glass chandelier hung from the ceiling. The room was very white. There was a rose-patterned carpet. I remember the building looking larger than it really is. I haven't been in there since Adrienne was in Berkeley.

Adrienne Kennedy would take me down the short road to the Men's Faculty Club (now called simply the Faculty Club), which is a Bernard Maybeck building. I thought about the music in Walt Disney's *Peter and the Wolf* where Peter escaped out of his grandfather's cabin towards the forest. It would be dark out and the lamps that hung from the wooden posts would shine on the cement making my shadows long and lean. I remember exploring the Faculty Club. The walls were made from the wood of Manchurian oaks.

Around the corner from the main dining room was a conference room, which I think was for the board of directors' meetings. The room was tucked in a corner on the northeast side of the building. I stood in the doorway to take a look at it. I remember the bright fluorescent lights shining in the empty room. The lights outside of the building streamed into the room because there was a window in the back that faced north. I could see the optometry building where I used to get my eyes examined. Twelve large, red leather chairs on wheels surrounded the long, oval-shaped conference table. I envisioned a room full of men sitting around the table, talking and looking at papers. I think a pot of roses sat in the middle of the table, but I'm not sure about that. For some reason, as I studied the conference room, I recalled the scene in Walt Disney's *Peter and the Wolf* where Peter meets the bird Sasha as he goes off to hunt the wolf. I thought of both the narration and the background music. I don't really know why I thought of that soundtrack. Maybe I had listened to it earlier that day or maybe there was something about the way the room was designed that started it playing in my head.

The Faculty Club retains a lot of meaning to me even now because of its connection to Adrienne Kennedy. All of us have had birthday parties there. I had my seventeenth, eighteenth and twentieth birthday parties there, either in the Clark Kerr Dining Room or the Great Hall. I have been to the Faculty Club many times since Adrienne Kennedy was in town, but I haven't seen the conference room since then. This was the first time I was around another writer who was special to me.

After a trip to Port Townsend, Washington, I started 1/2 at Park School in the fall of 1984. It was another hard year. I was not so little anymore and I began to become more aware of what was going on around me. I was seven and a half. The teachers this year didn't have any children of their own, which should have been a red flag. They were in their early thirties. One day we were assigned a cutting project. It was in the spring of 1985. I don't remember what the exact project was. The teachers were frustrated because I was having trouble. Their reaction was to laugh at me. I thought that they were laughing because they thought it was funny. Now, I think they were laughing because they were uncomfortable. I remember one of the teachers saying, "Look at how she cuts," and then making that awful, high-pitched laugh that showed nervousness and immaturity, a lethal combination. "That's the way she cuts," said the other teacher. "That's just the way she cuts." She was shaking her head out of frustration. I remember feeling embarrassed and looking at my classmates, who were concentrating on their projects and probably had not been aware of what was going on.

During Park School assemblies we had to sing a song called "Park School's Number One." It was mandatory for us to sing it but I felt awkward singing it because Park School was definitely not "Number One" to me. I sat there with my nose in the air. I don't think the teachers noticed this.

I also had problems with math. We were learning geometric shapes in the spring of 1985. I had the most difficult time with learning the shapes. I thought it was because the teachers were going too fast, but that wasn't it. I like to look at shapes. My favorite shape is the upside down equilateral triangle. I began to pay attention to it when I got my first Guess tee shirt and then when I went to Japan in 1996 and saw them smacked all over the windows of high-rise skyscrapers in Kyoto, Hiroshima, Nagoya, Fukuoka and Sapporo.

These teachers didn't know how to teach geography or history. They told us that Taiwan was an island east of Japan. They also told us that a peninsula is a horseshoe shaped piece of land where boats come in. That year was when I first learned about the Holocaust in Europe and about

Anne Frank. I learned that Anne Frank was born in Frankfurt, Germany, and immigrated to Amsterdam, The Netherlands. That was true. They told us she died in a gas chamber. That wasn't true. I visited the Anne Frank house when I went to Amsterdam in June of 1993. She died of typhoid fever at the Bergen Belsen concentration camp in Germany. The camp was liberated a few days after she passed away. I traveled to Germany and The Netherlands in 1992, 1993 and 1994.

I remember one very embarrassing moment that school year. It was a Wednesday afternoon, just before it was time for school to let out. I was looking forward to my dance and drama class. It was in November of 1984, and I was getting ready for a rehearsal of *The Nutcracker*. I saw the K/1 class let out for the day, so I thought my class was getting out. When I went outside I sat down on the long, colorful dragon. I don't know what material the dragon was made of, but it was a sculpture for us to play on. I realized that the K/1 class was the only one outside. Imani, a girl in my class, said, "Tennessee, you better get back in here," in a hostile voice. I returned. My teachers didn't say anything but I was so embarrassed.

I didn't like Imani. Imani had a bad attitude, not nearly as bad as Miranda R, but bad enough to make me dislike her. She was a troubled child. Unfortunately, she perpetuated the stereotype of the angry black female. Everyone in the class stayed away from her. I was grateful for my friends. My friends were Alexandra, Rebecca, Miranda T, Caitlin, Robin, Lauren, Miriam, and Caroline. I remember all of them coming to my eighth birthday party, which was on a Saturday evening in early March of 1985. I also remember going to their birthday parties. When Miranda R wasn't around they treated me better. Even though I had only five good friends out of a class of thirty they were always there for me. They didn't think badly of me because I had trouble in school. They were very patient. They were more of a teacher to me than the teachers were. Rebecca helped me sew my name on a brown cloth, which the class rabbit later chewed up. Alexandra had curly hair like me and we used to bite each other's curls. Miranda T was in The Children's Troupe for a year. We were in *Saint George and the Dragon* in the fall of 1986, when we were in fourth grade. We hung out a lot, especially because we appeared together in the play. Each weekend I was hanging out with any one of these girls.

I also remember that I wasn't as amused by my teachers' actions as my classmates were. Sometimes, in order to get our attention, one teacher would play the xylophone while the other teacher would dance. My classmates would find it amusing. I didn't think it was. I would just sit there and look at them like they were foolish and thinking about how much I didn't like them. I also felt embarrassed for them because of their immaturity.

The teachers would also mock us. The younger grades would go on an annual camping trip out in the East Bay, somewhere near Walnut Creek. The teachers of the younger grades would hold assemblies, demonstrating what not to do on the trip. The teacher during my first year came up close to us where a play fire had been lit and pretended like she was a little kid making this hideous sound (kind of like a ga-ga-goo-goo type thing) and walking like a monkey. She looked ridiculous. I was so embarrassed. While my schoolmates were laughing *with* them I was laughing *at* them. They kind of reminded me of cartoons and movies like *Dances with Wolves* or *Memoirs of a Geisha* where white people imitate Native-American culture, Asian-American or African-American culture with negative stereotypes all over the place. Here it was an adult trying to imitate a child, with a lot of negative stereotypes. I think they were trying to get the kids to pay attention by being amusing. A lot of my schoolmates were naïve because they went along with it, but you can't fault them because they were kids.

Park School tried to emphasize that they were liberal, but that was a façade. I participated in a Thanksgiving play and a Black History Month assembly, where there were a lot of negative stereotypes exhibited such as the Indians being grateful for the Pilgrims. They had the Indians giving them food and eating corn with them and talking in the style of the King James Version of the Bible. Martin Luther King Jr.'s "I Have A Dream" speech was about as much of the Civil Rights Movement that they knew. Now, when I go to a school or job or some other place where they say they are liberal, I put up a red flag immediately. Dad says to this day that Park School changed me for the worse. He thinks that I entered Park School as a friendly, cheerful and optimistic child and left it angry, combative and resentful. He remembers me saying after I left, "They were mean to me." Unfortunately, no school at the time would have been a good place for me to be.

I left Park Day School in June of 1985. The administration felt it was best for me because it wasn't working out. I didn't mind. I wanted to get out of there anyway. In December of 2007, I went to Park School's website and its motto is:

"Park Day School is a diverse, independent K–8 School with a thirty-year history of progressive education. We believe a successful learner is one who is confident, caring, and creative. We believe success is measured by a student's ability to define his or her place in the world, guided by intellectual skills and a social perspective." (www.parkdayschool.org)

Mind you, this is 2008 and I went to Park School between the fall of 1983 and the spring of 1985, but I think that motto hasn't changed much since I went there, especially the "progressive" part. What they say on the website is the exact opposite of my experience there. I also found out that my old teachers are still there.

Just like with Kaiser, I was supposed to stay at Park School until sixth grade. That didn't happen. I transferred out of the Oakland schools. I started going to school in Berkeley. The first school was Le Conte, a public primary school. I went there because my good friend Ms. Smith-Miller was going to teach my class. She was my afternoon daycare worker when I was two. She was my first African-American grade school teacher. At Le Conte my life began to change for the better. My language skills improved. I thought better of myself. It was the first time I ever smiled in a school picture. My hair was longer and prettier, and my clothes were better. My reading, writing, and math skills were excellent. I made a lot of good friends at Le Conte; in fact, I didn't have any problems with my classmates. This was in part because I wasn't insecure so my classmates were able to approach me and because my teacher and the principal used strict supervision. Ms. Smith-Miller was one of the best teachers I had, and therefore, she was a big influence for me. At the time she was getting her doctorate and she was training to become a principal.

Ms. Smith-Miller had us do a lot of work. I remember doing many book reports. This helped improve my language and writing skills. I went to a speech therapist, Mrs. McGee, whose son Skylar went to Park Day School at the same time as I and had transferred to Le Conte as well. He was a biracial black kid as well and he had learning disabilities. We were in the same class at Park Day and Le Conte. I felt better that I wasn't the only one who struggled at Park School. We read stories out loud and did some writing. I only got sick with one ear infection and strep throat. This led me to believe that stress had a detrimental effect on my health. The other school years (Pre-School–2nd grade), I had many ear infections, a mild form of the measles and viral croup.

When I was at Le Conte, I started participating in The Children's Troupe of Roberts and Blank. We had our rehearsals at a church designed by Julia Morgan off of Solano Avenue in Berkeley. I went there on Monday, Wednesday, and Friday after school. I felt nervous there at first. Taya, Tara, Molly and Julie were still there, and they were in seventh grade. I hung out with them a lot in the dressing room. One day I showed off my green and orange shimmer socks, which I wore with a sweatshirt, pants and white plastic flats, to Taya, Tara, Molly and Julie. I turned off the lights to show that they glowed in the dark.

I remember when we did our first set of performances of "Remy Charlip Meets The Children's Troupe" at the Florence Schwimley Little Theatre on the Berkeley High School Campus. My part was the punchline at the end of each scene. Mom says that The Children's Troupe needed a little bit of spice. I was the youngest in the group. I learned how to behave on stage by observing Taya, Tara, Molly and Julie and seeing how serious they were. I grew more confident by looking up to them. They accepted me into their group. I used to sit there and watch them rehearse. I learned good memory, concentration, multiple-step direction, motor, organization, public speaking, and language and communication-compensating skills from working in The Children's Troupe. I attended The Children's Troupe from the fall of 1985 through the spring of 1992 (grades three through nine). During those seven years I built up my self-esteem and self-confidence. I learned how to work with other people. Sometimes that was difficult, particularly in seventh and eighth grades, but I still managed. In the fall of 1985, not long after I joined The Children's Troupe, I stopped going to the doctor for ear infections so often. Instead of going twice a month like before, I went twice a year. The ear infections stopped all together when I was in fifth grade. Now I only get them if I travel on an airplane with a cold. I also stopped going to private speech and language therapy. I was healthier because I had more self-confidence. I also learned that sitting still, being quiet, and spitting out retained information was not my learning style. I was more of a hands-on learner.

I started piano lessons with Michael Margolis right before I turned nine. I studied classical music. First, I learned scales and fingering, but he really wanted me to learn to read music even though listening fits my learning style. Practicing the piano helped me improve my hand-eye skills by learning to work the finger muscles. My left hand hurt from having to strengthen it, but that only took a week. I don't remember what inspired me to start taking piano lessons but I enjoyed them. I took lessons on Thursday afternoons. I played Bach's "Minuets in G Major" and "Minuets in G Minor," classical folk songs and jazz music by Thelonious Monk, Miles Davis, Duke Ellington and Scott Joplin. When I was eleven, I traveled to Disneyland where I played the piano outside a restaurant. I got a very good reception. I also studied with Mary Watkins, the great jazz pianist, who is my dad's teacher.

In third grade I did my first poetry reading. We traveled to U.C. Santa Cruz where I read Dad's poem "Beware Do Not Read This Poem" either at the college bookstore or the library. I felt very nervous when I went up to the podium and saw all of the adults staring at me. I read very slowly to make sure that I didn't make any mistakes. I managed though. In January of 1986 we went on our second trip to Alaska where Dad attended the First Annual Alaska Native Publishing Company conference. I read on Alaska Public Radio. I don't remember what poem I read. From then on I traveled around the world reading my poetry.

Another great thing about Le Conte was the principal, Dr. Penny-James, who recently retired. She was at Le Conte for at least eighteen years. She was excellent. She also enforced the rules consistently on students. Le Conte was the only school where I felt safe around both the students and the teachers. Dr. Penny-James had transferred to Arts Magnet in 1998, where she stayed until she retired. She was well known throughout Berkeley. All of my family friends who worked in the Berkeley Public Schools knew about her and said great things about her, like longtime family friend Elaine Overstreet, who my parents knew from the New York days. She worked at both Martin Luther King Junior High School and Oxford Elementary School. Miss Ruckers also worked at Le Conte School starting in 1980 and said that Dr. Penny-James made a huge impression on Le Conte parents, teachers and students.

My Le Conte School classroom had students from other countries. One girl was from Samoa, and the boys made fun of her because she was large. Her name was Laot. That ended quickly thanks to Ms. Smith-Miller. She didn't tolerate bullying. Laot was nice to me. I liked her smile. There was one girl from Japan named Misato and two Taiwanese girls named Wei-Shin and Jenny. I was one of the few students who spoke with them on a regular basis. I have always been comfortable around people from other countries.

I left Le Conte School in the spring of 1986 because Le Conte only went to third grade at the time. There was a little commencement ceremony where they showed a video of the third grade trip to Camp Cazadero near the Russian River in Guerneville. In the fall of 1995 the Berkeley Public Schools changed. Before the school district had K–3, 4–6, 7–8 and 9–12 schools. Now the schools go from K–5, 6–8 and then 9–12. Berkeley High is the only public high school in Berkeley. During that school year I had to figure out what school I wanted to go to for fourth through sixth grades. I was going to go Malcolm X but then I decided on John Muir because my best friend, Jessica, was going to go there. Jessica and I stayed at John Muir from fourth through sixth grades. She had a younger brother and sister. We stayed in touch through eleventh grade. We lost touch because of what was going on in her life. Last I heard she'd become a born-again Christian and got married. She lives in Sacramento.

Fourth Through Sixth Grade

N BETWEEN THIRD AND FOURTH GRADE WE TRAVELED TO OAHU, Hawaii for two weeks where I met poet and good friend Kathryn Takara. Kathryn taught in the English Department at the University of Hawaii at Manoa in Honolulu. I met her older daughter, Karla Brundage, who was going to turn nineteen that August and was a student at Vassar College. She got her teaching credentials at San Francisco State in 1998 while she taught at a private Catholic school in Honolulu. Karla is also a poet and she now teaches at the Athenian School in Danville. Dad published her book, *Swallowing Watermelons*. My mom edited it. In 2001, Karla taught on a Fulbright Scholarship in Zimbabwe. She took her daughter, Asha, who was seven at the time, with her. In 2003 Karla and Asha moved to Oakland because Karla got a job teaching at Albany High School for two years before going to Athenian. I speak with Karla frequently, as she has invited me to several events and I invite her to read as well. She recited her poetry at my campaign fundraising event in 2008 where both Cynthia McKinney and I spoke. Reginald Lockett, Oakland's late poet laureate, was the first to sign on to read at the event. He died about a week after the event. I was running for the School Board District One in Oakland, and Representative Cynthia McKinney spoke about her quest to become Green Party nominee for president. Her endorsing me was one of the highlights of my political career, which was in its infancy. I ran for office because I wanted to be an advocate for students who are having the same problems that I had, like black, Latino and learning disabled students. I read at several Hurricane Katrina fundraising events in the fall of 2005 and the fall of 2006. We also read at San Jose State University, in a reading that featured poets whom Dad had published. In addition to us, there was Boadiba and Nell Moody.

I also met Kathryn's younger daughter, Natasha Takara. Natasha was ten when I met her but she was going to turn eleven in November. She was going to enter sixth grade in the fall of 1986. In June of 1991 we took Natasha to New York where she got her first look at a big city. We stayed at the Southgate Tower Hotel, across the street from Madison Square Garden. We visited places like the Metropolitan Museum of Art in Manhattan and the Cloisters in the Bronx. We went to see a Broadway musical about the famous comedian Will Rogers called *The Will Rogers Follies*, a Tony Award-winning musical with a book by Peter Stone, lyrics by Betty Comden and Adolph Green, and music by Cy Coleman. Norman Schwarzkopf was at the musical. I remember at intermission someone saying, "Ladies and Gentlemen: Norman Schwarzkopf." Everyone clapped his or her hands except for Natasha and Mom.

In August of 1991, I went to Hawaii for a week to stay with them as a "thank you" present from Kathryn. I was going into ninth grade and Natasha was going to be in eleventh grade. Natasha went to Stanford University where she met her future husband, Brad. She lived in Seattle for a few years. She has lived in Oakland since 2004 and has a three-year-old daughter named Makayla. She is expecting a baby boy around Christmas-time. Before I started having chronic pain, I used to take walks with her, Makayla and Pronto the Dog in the Oakland hills. She and I are only fifteen months apart in age.

I began fourth grade at John Muir School in Berkeley in the fall of 1986. This was another good school for me. My teacher, Ms. Ash (who got married in the middle of the semester and changed her name to Mrs. O'Kelly) was a teacher who also believed in making us work hard. She had a huge map of the United States on the wall that helped me a little on my geography. My dad introduced me to geography when I was very little. He'd have me identify the countries on a map located in the downstairs bathroom. He referred to Africa as "Mother Africa." I read maps before I read books. The map moved to my bedroom in 2002 when the bathroom was painted. It is located above the desk where my electronics sit.

Mrs. O' Kelly wasn't the kind of teacher who taught us only European history. She taught us about Native Americans, Africans, Asians, and

Latinos. I only remember one incident where she yelled at me in public. It was during English class. The class stared at me, and Emily, my friend, looked shocked. I was too surprised to say anything. This only happened one time. She was a good teacher.

I enjoyed science. It became my favorite subject. The only homework I remember Mrs. O'Kelly giving were assignments that we didn't finish during the school day. I only stayed one semester with her because during the second semester I lived in Massachusetts. Dad was invited to teach a semester at Harvard University in Cambridge by Werner Sollors, who was then the department head of African-American Studies.

In the fall of 1986 I participated in two performances. One was named *Saint George and the Dragon*, with The Children's Troupe. The other was *Manifest Destiny* that Mom and I performed in at Laney College in early November of 1986. We both wore long, shimmer-gold strapless dresses. Mom wore silver high-top sneakers, like the shoes that boxers wear. I wore blue tights, red socks and white high-top Reeboks. I had my hair in two French braids and red, white and blue ribbons hung from my gold crown. Portia and Rebecca put my makeup on. I remember how hard it was for me to sit still while mascara was being applied. Both Portia and Rebecca wore all black because they were stagehands.

Manifest Destiny was a dance theater piece Mom started in 1986. She did lots of research about the politics and iconography that was used to explain or justify our becoming an American Empire, starting in the eighteenth and nineteenth centuries. It was common then to have female images represent America. The goddesses were called Columbia or Liberty, and they appeared on historical and legal documents, as ship mastheads, weather vanes, and as sculptures and paintings. In many of them, the women were designed to look like a combination of a Greek goddess and some romanticized idea of an Indian maiden.

For one scene, Mom and I made up a duet, set to "The Rose Has a Thorn," by Chris Planas, who would later appear playing guitar on "For All We Know," a recording by the Ishmael Reed Quintet. We performed the kind of dances that were popular in nineteenth-century American pageants. We dressed as Columbia and Little Liberty, in our gold *lamé* mother/daughter dresses. Mom had a U.S. flag draped around her shoulders and I waved a little flag on a stick. Later Mom transformed into an eagle and rescued me so I got to fly across the stage. Actually, I was hooked to a special gizmo they use in the theater, the kind of contraption that makes it possible for Peter Pan to fly. The audience went "Oooh! Aaaah!" I couldn't see them because the bright lights on the stage made the house look pitch black.

The scene I remember the most was me standing on top of a lit platform holding a torch. Mom was in the back, changing into her next costume. I remember the quote from Ronald Reagan, "Homeless people like being homeless. Hungry people don't know any better." He was still president at the time. I remember trying hard not to laugh. I don't know why I thought that quote was so funny.

After the performance I was excited. *Manifest Destiny* was a great learning experience because I learned about American history in a way that I wasn't learning in school. It was a hands-on history lesson for me. I don't think I will ever forget performing *Manifest Destiny*, like I will never forget performing any of the plays I did in The Children's Troupe.

In mid-December I participated in *Saint George and the Dragon*. We performed at the Florence Schwimley Little Theatre. The "Saint George and the Dragon" legend originates in the Middle Ages, and it shows some influences from the crusades in the Middle East. Miranda T and I both wore leotards and blue baggy pants. We sat cross-legged inside of the night sky cloth, while Tara dragged us across the stage. We sang an original Christmas carol called "Luly Lula." Miranda T and I played the part of the two-headed dragon.

At the same time Mom and Jody managed with The Children's Troupe they worked with children in the Berkeley Public Schools. In the fall of 1986, they worked with Columbus Elementary School in West Berkeley (now called Rosa Parks School). The children in this class were eleven-years-old and in sixth grade, which means they were born in 1975. Since I was very little, I have been interested in the lives of older people. The Columbus School group did a play called *Come Back, Jimmy Mack*, using the song by Martha Reeves and the Vandellas. It was a variation on the mummer's plays.

I remember the class in detail. The teacher was Chinese-American, in her mid-forties. I never talked to her but I could tell she was the exception to the rule when it came to teachers I'd had, because she encouraged creativity in the classroom. The kid who was supposed to play "Jimmy Mack" had broken his leg and was on crutches. He would dash across the stage and sometimes fall. His name was Josh. This girl, Amy, would run to him and ask, "Are you all right?' That was the first time I had seen a crush going on. I also remember how far ahead of the times this group was because the choir introduced both plays with a rap. I didn't really interact with the Columbus School group that much, even though we shared a dressing room and rehearsal time. We all performed three times during the day and once at night. The performances were from Monday through Thursday during the week before our Christmas vacation.

The one girl I focused on was an African-American named Trisha. She was tall and thin. I liked her style of clothes. On the Thursday, our last day, she wore a wide striped black and white sweater with a multi-colored striped shirtsleeve tee underneath, a light bluejean mini-skirt, white nylon tights and white and yellow Reebok sneakers. She had her shoulder-length hair in multiple braids with red ribbons. In the evening, she changed her top to a white blouse and a black velvet vest. That look fascinated me even though it was a classic outfit. The Columbus School group was required to wear white, black and a little bit of red.

Trisha was very nice to me. There was something about her that was trustworthy, even though I didn't know her that well. She was quiet and focused, a personality I wished I had. I was really envious that she was able to pick out her clothes and put on her stage make-up without any help in front of the long and wide mirror.

I remember Trisha doing the "Jimmy Mack" dance on stage and making the "oops" face when she missed a step. She also performed the "This Little Light of Mine" dance, where the stage was so dark the dancers looked like they were in shadow. Every time I listen to "Jimmy Mack" on the iPod I think of Trisha. When I also listen to "How Will I Know" by Whitney Houston I also think of Trisha since it came out in 1986. I also remember her friend Arlene. She was in the chorus. When I got to Cambridge Mom and I took the T to Boston where I got the same blue jean mini-skirt and the same Reeboks Trisha had. I wore my bluejean mini-skirt and Reeboks with my penguin sweatshirt, my Esprit logo sweatshirt or my Guess logo tee and white turtleneck and thick, white cotton tights. I often wonder if the people in that class remember *Come Back, Jimmy Mack*. They are all thirty-three now and are my best friend Natasha's age. I googled Trisha's name and found out that she acted in the 2008 mini-series, *The Capture of the Green River Killer*, carried on the Lifetime network.

Life in Massachusetts was excellent. While I was living there in the spring of 1987, I wrote a lot of poems. We stayed in a condominium that was part of a mansion that was once owned by the former chief of the town's waterworks. Martha Nussbaum, a classics professor and author, rented her condominium to us. One day a crew from *Esquire* magazine came and photographed Dad modeling an Armani sweater. It was a two-story apartment. Downstairs there was a study/guest bedroom where I typed on the typewriter, a kitchen, a bathroom, a living room and a dining room. Upstairs were my bedroom, a long hallway, my parents' room and the bathroom. I rode the school bus to Agassis School, a public K–8 school in Cambridge, every morning. Mrs. Hart, our teacher, didn't believe in giving us extra homework, but if we didn't finish our math in class we would do it at home.

One of the things I remembered about living there was my class taking swimming lessons on Monday mornings at Harvard University. That stopped around March, so then I swam on Thursday after school. At home I watched *Square One*, a math show, and *3-2-1 Contact*, a science show. My step-grandfather, Bennie S. Reed, Sr., had a mild stroke while he and my grandmother, Thelma Virginia Reed, drove from Buffalo to visit. I don't remember him collapsing. I just remember the paramedics coming. He died in 1992, but Grandma still blames him for the stroke. She says he shouldn't have driven such a long distance.

DEATH CALLED MY GRANDFATHER

In 1988,
when my parents went to Europe,
I visited my grandparents in Buffalo.
My cousin, little Vincent,
was two years old.
You can't tell he has heart trouble.
He started hitting on me
and then my grandfather said,
"Keep it up and I'll whip you."
(That was a threat, not a promise.)

Little Vincent started
hitting on him
and then my grandfather went
looking for a belt
and he said
he couldn't find it.

I was upstairs in my room,
and it was so hot
that I couldn't go to sleep,
and I was reading *Superfudge*,
the part where Peter's brother, Fudge, was missing,
and Fudge's bird, who was name Uncle Feather,
said "Bonjour stupid,"
and Peter said, "Oh, shut up."
Uncle Feather said, "Shut up yourself, yourself, yourself,"
and I ran down the stairs, cracking up.

I was hyper, I don't know why.
I think it must have been the Buffalo weather,
and I read Grandpa the story
and after that,
Grandpa always answered the phone,
when I would say, "Hello,"
with "Shut up yourself, yourself, yourself,"
and we'd giggle together.

Death called my grandfather
cause he had cancer
in his lungs

and his stomach.
(This was real, not fake.)

When I saw him next
he was in a coffin
with a new suit on
and his face made up.
I remember that.

I remember
when we got there,
the night before the funeral,
I was tired from traveling,
but I couldn't sleep
because I was nervous,
and I was in a strange place,
and it was totally black,
so I couldn't see
anything.

I remember the minister
preaching about the Lord.
He said, "Death is not a stop.
It's a yield sign."

And getting my suede shoes
messed up
in the yucky mud
of the graveyard.

And everybody standing
under umbrellas
on a cold, wintry day
listening to what
the preacher was saying:
"Ashes to ashes
dust to dust."

The last thing I remember
of my grandfather
is standing by his coffin
and walking back
to the black limousine
to ride back to the church

with my 5 cousins,
his grandchildren.

I also hung out with an old family friend named Dorothy Hansberry. I had met her at Dartmouth when I was three or four but didn't remember her. She was the one who bought me my first Guess clothes. To this day I still wear Guess everyday. Mom was trying hard not to get me into brand names. For my twelfth birthday I got a Guess sweatshirt from Dorothy that was red, white and navy blue. At the time I didn't really care about Guess. That was in the back of my mind. I liked the Guess logo with the triangle and the question mark. I stayed at Dorothy's house during the day my first week in Massachusetts while I looked for schools and she bought me these clothes. She also bought me red and white slippers to go along with my red and white bathrobe. I spent many weekends with her. I kept that logo tee for five years.

I enjoyed going to the Harvard Museum of Natural History. I loved the llamas there. Mrs. Hart also took us aboard the Mayflower ship, to Old Plymouth and to Thompson Island, a private island in the Boston Harbor Islands National Park area. I learned a lot of stuff about New England while I was there. I remember women dressed as pilgrims walking around Old Plymouth in a staged pilgrim town that had a long dirt road. I didn't know much about New England history. I asked if they were real pilgrims. A boy thought I was crazy but Mrs. Hart wasn't upset at all about the question. I started reading *The Baby-sitter's Club* in Massachusetts. I first read *Claudia and the Phantom Phone Caller*, which was the second book in the series. The author was Ann M. Martin. I just ran into it by accident in the class bookshelves. Now my second cousins who are nine, ten and twelve are reading the series.

At Agassis School, I met my very good friend, Heather. She was the one who really helped me adjust to my new environment. Her parents are both Japanese-American and are from Hawaii. Heather lived in Cambridge for her entire fourth-grade year. She was born in Madison, Wisconsin and moved to the Bay Area when she was four. At the time she and her family were based in San Jose. When we were in sixth grade, she moved to Fremont, California. Both in Cambridge and in the Bay Area we hung out a lot. Her father worked as a professor at a Divinity School in Berkeley, so she came up to Berkeley where we went swimming at Strawberry Canyon or hung out at my house. Sometimes she spent the night with us or I spent the night in Fremont or San Jose. We also attended a summer sports camp in 1991 at U.C. Berkeley. She came with me to my middle school's semi-formal dance as seventh grade came to a close.

Heather attended U.C. Santa Cruz for college and California State University, East Bay for graduate school where she majored in English as a Second Language. Heather worked in Bangkok, Thailand from the fall of 2005 through the spring of 2007. In September of 2007 she left for Thailand again, where she teaches English.

We moved back to the Bay Area in the summer of 1987. I was glad to come back because I missed California. I missed my friend and neighbor Niecy Harris, who was my very best friend, and my cats Happy and Apricot. We had a very unpleasant surprise when we returned. A crack operation had just started on our street. I would hear gunshots and people shouting and arguing in the middle of the night. My window faced the street. That was when I lived downstairs. My dad informed the Oakland Police about the situation. They told me to sleep in the kitchen on the first and fifteenth of each month because sometimes innocent people were injured by bullets penetrating through the windows facing the street. Dad started the Neighborhood Crime Watch and the police were afraid that the dealers would retaliate against us because of this. This operation went on for at least two years. I finally moved upstairs in the summer of 1994. I am still facing the street and there are still drug dealings going on. In December of 2006 there was a full-scale shoot out that took place on the block. There were .45 calibre bullets lying all over the street after the exchange of fire. The gunshots penetrated the homes and cars of our neighbors. Dad wrote an article about this shooting in *Playboy*. It was titled "Assisted Homicide in Oakland." I take painkillers before I go to sleep, which makes me not hear anything now.

While I was away in Cambridge my neighbor across the street and Niecy had made friends with two girls who lived next door to her house. They were the same age as us. They had a black mother and a white stepfather. I didn't like them. When I was fourteen and in ninth grade the stepfather sent a letter and a Christmas card to me. Dad was livid. In the letter he criticized my parents for not permitting me to play with him. My father felt that the letter included passages of a sexual nature. He was trying to lure me into a relationship with him. My father sent a caustic warning to him, demanding that he stop sending such letters.

My father consulted his lawyer, Howard Moore Jr., about what could be done. Mr. Moore told him "not much." My parents decided to form a protective shield between the man and me. We had little trouble from him after that. One day, when I was fifteen and in tenth grade, we noticed TV trucks and reporters all over the block. A bloodhound was sniffing around his house. He was a suspect in the kidnapping and murdering three girls. The Christmas card he sent me had a picture of a four-year old Russian girl, who looked very much like one of the kidnapped girls. The man had tried to make friends with the girls across the street who had just moved in 1997 or 1998. He was never arrested and the case remains open. A book about the murders called *Stalemate* by psychologist John Philpin was published in 1997. The man and his family moved out of our neighborhood in 2005 or 2006.

I attended John Muir School again for fifth grade in the fall of 1987. My teacher, Mrs. Spatz, also believed in hard work. She would assign us an essay every Monday and it would be due on Friday. I enjoyed doing the essays. This was the year when I learned how to add, subtract, multiply, and divide fractions with both the same and different denominators. I don't remember having trouble. In the afternoons she read us *Superfudge* by Judy Blume while we did our secret writing. Secret writing was when we wrote privately in our composition notebooks and the teachers put on music or read to us to help us relax enough to write. Sometimes we stuck our binders up so others couldn't see our writing. That happened right after lunch to calm us down after we ran around. I enjoyed that part of the day because that was the only time of day I could express my creativity. She put our desks in different groups in terms of categories at the beginning of each month. She was also a teacher who believed in helping with my disability. I enjoyed her a lot. I missed her when I left fifth grade. She transferred to Jefferson School in Berkeley before she retired.

In October, my good friend Subira enrolled at John Muir. Subira's birthday was in November, so she was still nine when she entered John Muir. I talked with her when the class took a walk across the Golden Gate Bridge to celebrate the bridge's fiftieth anniversary. That's when I got to know her. She was angry about her experiences in her former school. She called the teachers "airheads." After that we hung out at recess and at my home and hers. We swam at Strawberry Canyon together. After we graduated from sixth grade we hung out occasionally. In ninth and tenth grades we barely talked. In eleventh grade I went to a play at Holy Names High School that she appeared in and we were reunited. I don't remember the play, but David S, my friend from the private high school I attended, Arrowsmith Academy, was also in the play. In 1998 she helped me move into the Clark Kerr Dormitory when I transferred to U.C. Berkeley from Laney Community College. I saw her this past October in New York City.

Subira was born in the Bronx. She moved to Oakland when she was two or three. Subira attended Spellman College in Atlanta. She got her degree in International Relations. During her junior year in college she spent a semester in South Africa. She stayed in Atlanta for a couple of years after graduation and then she moved to New York to work for *W* magazine. My dad had encouraged her to become a journalist after publishing an article about South Africa by her in his magazine *Konch*. She has traveled all over the world. I think the only continent she hasn't been to is Antarctica.

From December 10–27, 1987 we traveled to Martinique, a small island in the Caribbean Ocean in between Dominique and Saint Lucia. I had been to Martinique before right before I turned eight in January of 1985, again for two and a half weeks. We traveled there both times because my dad was invited to lecture at the University of the Antilles at Martinique by Veronique Vautor who was a professor at the University of Fort de France, which is the capital city. His reception during the second visit was chilly because a black woman in New York had told one Veronique's students that he hated black women. The origin of this rumor was a student to whom he had offered a good deal of valuable time, assisting her in a paper about his novel *Mumbo Jumbo*. He considered her ungrateful.

Since my last trip to Martinique in 1987, Veronique had remarried and changed her last name to Tarrieu. She had another daughter in 1989 who is now nineteen. They lived in a town called Schoelcher, which is where we stayed. I enjoyed Veronique's two older kids Jessica and Tobias. They were fourteen and seventeen. On the first trip, I mostly swam in swimming pools. There was a posh five-star hotel that included a swimming pool. It was surrounded by stones and tropical flowers. A stone balcony overlooked the sea to the west. No one questioned us as to whether or not we were guests when we walked onto their grounds. We usually took Jessica with us. I don't know the name of the town where this hotel was located.

Even though the Caribbean Sea was strange to me I was not uncomfortable swimming and surfing in it. Tobias tried to amuse us by using the surfboard as a scooter while we went windsurfing. It tipped over and we all landed in the water. I landed under the sail, but I wasn't scared. Every afternoon we went to the beach and windsurfed. Sometimes they took their four dogs with us. If I remember correctly, two of the dogs were Labs and two were German Shepherds. They swam in the shallow area. They didn't like being hosed. I remember them shaking the water off. I also hung out with the three cats. On Christmas Eve I brought over my toy mechanical mouse. The cats didn't know what to make of it. They would paw it and when it would flip over they would pull their paws away. That went on for a long time. I spent the night at their home a few times. Tobias and Jessica spoke both in French and English in front of me. They cussed in English in front of me one time and I laughed.

Jessica brought me with her to school to talk about the United States. I wore my new plaid Martinique dress with white lacy socks and some red German-made flats that Mom bought me at a children's shoe store called

Kinder Schuhe (German for children's shoes) on Rose Street and Shattuck Avenue in Berkeley. Mom used to buy all of my ergonomic shoes there. It doesn't exist anymore. The students in this class were freshmen and sophomores in high school. They gave me chocolates and a dozen roses. I remember talking about the education system in the United States, my travels around the country and the differences between each city I had visited. I talked about my semester in Cambridge, and about my friends back home as well.

I also remember visiting the house of a Martinique couple. They had two boys around my age and a two-year-old girl. I don't remember much about the kids or the couple. I really remember the ram in the neighbors' yard. He was a beautiful reddish-brown color and he had dark eyes. The ram paced back and forth in the backyard on a chained leash.

The people and I clicked, however the landscape and I didn't. The trip was exhausting. Martinique wasn't a popular destination back then. In fact, it was hard to find Martinique on the map. We had to fly on four or five planes to get there from San Francisco International Airport even on the major airlines like Pan Am, American and Air France. We had to stop in Dallas/Fort Worth, New York, San Juan, Saint Thomas, Saint Croix and Guadeloupe. The exhaustion from the traveling plus the jetlag made my panic attacks worse. I don't think the fact that I didn't speak French had anything to do it. I traveled to the Netherlands and Germany and I didn't have panic attacks in those countries. People thought that my age had to do with my problems in Martinique but I don't think it was that. I don't think I would enjoy Martinique at any age. It was hot and humid. I'm from northern California and I don't do well in that kind of weather. At least in places like Orlando, Washington, Philadelphia, New York, Boston, Frankfurt and Tokyo I had air-conditioning. In Martinique there wasn't any of that. It was also too rural for me. I'm a city girl.

Once I was back home, I started seeing a therapist at Kaiser Hospital Behavioral Medicine in 1988, due to the panic attacks I experienced in Martinique. I stopped seeing her in 1996 when I left pediatrics. My parents thought she helped me a lot with my problems even though I didn't see it that way and I still don't feel like she helped me much. I felt like I was being ganged up on by both my parents and my therapist. I felt like my opinion didn't matter to them and I felt that they weren't listening to me. They would get angry or irritated at anything I had to say. The therapist was inconsistent about the rules. She let my parents do things that she wouldn't allow me to do, like interrupting them. When I became a teenager I had a harder time with my therapist. I didn't agree with some of the things she recommended, like taking antibiotics for my acne even though my mother told her that I was very allergic to antibiotics. She told my mother that antibiotics were the only way to treat the acne. I was on a very toxic one called Accutane, whose side effects include severe sunburn, suicidal thoughts and liver damage. Basically I couldn't expose myself to the sun, the heat, the wind or the cold, because I would get blotchy red skin on my face, which looked more ugly than the acne. I was also put on topical antibiotics that could have contributed to melanoma because I was prone to sunburn. I think my therapist was trying to help me with my self-image, but since she wasn't a medical doctor she really didn't have the knowledge to tell me the cause of acne and how to treat it. She told me that I had to stop eating chocolate. While looking over a pamphlet about acne from Kaiser I read that no one really knew what caused acne, that antibiotics shouldn't be overused because they caused long term damage and that washing the face everyday was the best way to fight it. Time was going to heal it.

When I attended a summer sports camp at Cal during the summers of 1990 and 1991 the therapist told Mom to sign me up for a team sport. She was trying to get me out of my shell. She had worked with me for a few years by then and I still felt she didn't understand me. If she had known me she would have realized that I never liked team sports because I was often subjected to ridicule because of my hand-eye motor problem. The Children's Troupe was the best place for me to learn how to interact with others.

When I was in high school I challenged her when she told me to assimilate into the white male culture. She quickly changed the subject. I told her the Jim Crow era was over. This was another example of adults thinking they knew what was best for me and they really didn't. My therapist did not have the expertise to work with disabled children, nor the physical, behavioral and emotional symptoms and sensitivities that go along with the disabilities. She often shrugged off my sensitivities with frustration and a self-righteous attitude. Her ideas for helping me did not work with my specific problems. Therefore, she did not work for me. My parents should have taken me to a therapist who worked with children who had non-apparent disabilities, particularly learning disabilities, ADHD and chronic pain. Right now I work with a therapist who specializes in patients with chronic pain.

I had one major incident in fifth grade. There was a group of black girls that had some hostility towards me for being biracial. The girls shouted racial epithets, spat in my face, slapped me and verbally assaulted me, saying things like, "mother fucker" and "fucking retard." I returned fire, calling them "ugly black bitches." What would they have made of the fact that both Booker T. Washington and Frederick Douglass, and other great black leaders, men and women had white fathers? I'm not sure where they picked up this unattractive behavior, but I'm guessing they learned cues up from their parents when they were still in the pre-school age. Some of the teachers enabled their behaviors. I normally don't hit people, but since words didn't work in this situation, and the teachers weren't doing anything, I had to stand up for myself. I wasn't little anymore, so there was no excuse for me to let these girls continue to bully me.

A major incident happened in our science class. I don't remember how the incident started or what words were said. But this girl smacked me in the face. I was about to cry, but decided to defend myself after my science teacher teased me about getting slapped. "Boy, she's too sensitive," she said. The girl's friends were laughing, so I punched her. My classmates were shocked.

Things got so bad between these girls and me that when my friend Subira became friends with them, I was worried that she would start rejecting me as well. I got angry with her and told her, "You have to be friends with me or you have to be friends with them. It can't be both." She got angry with me for this and I called her a "fucking bitch." I was also angry with her because I felt she was too smart to hang around those girls. One day when I got into a fight with one of these nasty girls, Subira got angry with me and did not talk to me for two days.

In the spring of 1988, my first book of poetry *Circus in the Sky* was published. I had just turned eleven the week before. I received a lot of good comments from my classmates, even from one of the girls I'd fought with. I read at Cody's Bookstore and at Cafe Milano in Berkeley. I also won first place for my grade level in the Dulci Jubilo contest, a Berkeley poetry contest.

After a busy but wonderful summer, during which I got my ears pierced, I entered sixth grade again at John Muir in the fall of 1988. This is when I began to fall apart again. The hormones started their intensity and my first menstrual period was not far down the road. Our teacher was a rookie and she was totally inexperienced about how to deal with conflicts in the classroom. She also focused too much on the standardized tests, which weren't going to happen until the end of May or early June of 1989. She started preparing us in November of 1988. By the time we were going to take the tests I had been sick of them. I already had been sick of them after our second week of preparation. Because she was getting us ready for these tests, her teaching method was so vague and fast that I didn't really learn anything.

She didn't work us that hard. I had harder work between third through fifth grades. In those grades I paid attention and got good grades because I was challenged. I didn't feel challenged in sixth grade. Instead, I got distracted by what was going on in the classroom. I would pass notes to my friends and get into conflicts with people. I would also draw or write poems while she lectured. I was bored. I felt like I was too smart to be in that class. I remember I wanted to move on to middle school for sixth grade to a small private school named New Age Academy, where the teachers had years of experience. Mom was thinking about transferring me to New Age during the second semester, but she decided to wait until I was in seventh grade because I would have trouble adjusting so quickly.

All that teacher did was lecture us about how to learn to get along with one another when a conflict arose. These talks weren't really effective because there continued to be altercations in the classroom. It was quite obvious she didn't know what she was doing. I was sent to the principal's office a lot for fighting and yelling at my tormentors. Our teacher lived in a fantasy world. If she lived in reality she would have realized that her strategies fell on deaf ears. I was never going to get along with those girls and vice versa. Just like with most teachers, she would not call people on their behavior. She had no backbone and the kids could smell her fear. That gave them a sense of power. She let them walk all over her.

I had a lot of trouble with a girl named Amber this year. Now that I am older it has become obvious to me that she wanted to be accepted as being black just like I did. She was very fair skinned, even lighter than me, with golden hair and light brown eyes. She also had some learning disabilities herself. She called me a "zebra" and an "Oreo."

I ended up getting into a fight with Amber in the middle of the spring of 1989. They didn't get the message the year before when I punched out Nikia. My anger had been escalating since fourth grade. I said something nasty to Amber because she had called me a "zebra." I called her some four letter words and I also called her "an ugly black bitch." She spat in my face. I dug my nails into her skin. She spat on me again and then when she turned her back to me I pulled her by the hair.

Mom received a call from the principal, whose rules I thought were ridiculous, such as if you were five minutes late you would get detention. He also had these signs put up in each classroom that said, "Pay attention, follow directions and ask permission." He said to everyone that if we followed these rules we wouldn't get suspended. His rules were trivial to me. There were more important things that should have been done in order to keep the classroom a safe and pleasant environment, like kicking those girls out of school. I wasn't feeling safe. He didn't seem to care about that. I had sleep deprivation and dreaded going to school. That principal wasn't a terribly bright man. I never saw him observe the classrooms like Dr. Ilita-White and Dr. Penny-James. He didn't really understand our situation.

I got to finally graduate from sixth grade on June 20, 1989 with awards in Math and Science. I also won the Dulci Jubilo contest, getting the first place prize for my grade level again. The award was given to fourth through sixth graders in the Berkeley Public Schools for poetry, essays and short stories about the city of Berkeley. This was the second time I had received this award.

CHAPTER FIVE

Seventh Through Ninth Grade

I N BETWEEN SIXTH AND SEVENTH GRADE WE LIVED IN SEATTLE, Washington, one of the most beautiful cities in the country, for six weeks. Dad was invited to the University of Washington at Seattle by novelist Charles Johnson. Dad taught a class in poetry and my mother taught a theater class. We lived in the home of poet Heather McHugh. In my bedroom there was a huge Hershey Bar poster on the wall. I wrote a poem based on the poster called, "Electric Chocolate" and that's where the title of my second poetry collection, *Electric Chocolate* came from. In the summer of 1990, when *Electric Chocolate* came out, I sent a copy to Heather McHugh, who in return sent me the poster.

ELECTRIC CHOCOLATE

First Piece
I like Hershey's chocolate
bars because they are
rich and creamy. I imagine
that the tree in our front
yard is growing Hershey's.
The telephone poles and wires
are made of Hershey's. I
pretend I go out and
pick them off the tree. The
poles are chocolate wood.
The wires are electric chocolate.
Hershey's milk chocolate bars.

Second Piece
I wish I saw Hershey's everywhere.
I wish my house was made of Hershey's.
I wish I slept in Hershey's bed.
I wish I swam in chocolate water.
I wish I was made of chocolate color.

I wish this was Hershey's writing.
I wish the world was made of Hershey's.

I remember that the hormones seemed to be more intense for me when I got to Seattle. I was unhappy with the short haircut that my mother decided would be more convenient for her. There was no length to it. According to a hairdresser it is not feminine-looking when women cut their hair too short.

The intense hormonal changes got worse after I had recently started menstruating. I went to summer camp from 8:30–4:30 from Monday through Friday at the University of Washington at Seattle. In the morning we had English and then Drama. After lunch we had Art and then swimming. Then we hung out until our parents came. We sometimes visited the Burke Museum of Natural History and Culture, which was on campus.

There were two really nasty girls there. They were twelve and ten. We got into verbal confrontations almost all of the time about nearly everything. The teachers let them get away with their bad behavior. I was a good friend with a girl named Kendra who was ten. I focused on her more than I did the other girls. I really enjoyed the drama and swimming classes but I didn't care for the Art and English classes. I could tell that my art teachers didn't like my style of art.

On the weekends, I hung out with Elizabeth Johnson, Charles Johnson's seven-year-old daughter. We used to play in the backyard of the home I was staying in or I would go over to her house. In 1996 I wrote her a note saying that I was going down to Claremont College in southern California because Dad was going to a conference. I was nineteen and she was fourteen. At the last minute Charles Johnson booked her on a Southwest Airlines flight from Seattle to Ontario since he was going down there himself. We went swimming in the pool at Scripps College. Later on I took her to dinner at a restaurant in downtown. She also went with me to get a second hole pierced in both of my ears. At her hotel room, I remember her saying that the boys couldn't believe that both of her parents were black since she had sandy hair, light skin and blue eyes. We listened to D'Angelo and Hootie and the Blowfish.

Seeing that I needed a small classroom environment, Mom enrolled me at Berkeley's New Age Academy in the fall of 1989 for seventh grade. It was a private middle school with only twenty-one students. At the time there were only four seventh-graders. The head teacher and principal was an upper-class African-American from Philadelphia who didn't believe in learning disabilities. Instead she believed that people learned differently, or so my parents and I thought. In 2007 I researched the New Age Academy online and this was what I found:

"My mission is to support world peace by creating and nurturing learning environments that foster intellectual, emotional, and spiritual growth for adolescents, teachers, and community members." (www.newageacademy.net.)

If she had followed her mission, the school would have been a perfect place. However, she was angry on the surface. But now that I am older I can see that her anger stemmed from fear. She did not know how to deal with students like me. She got frustrated because she thought that her methods of teaching worked for everyone and she got hurt because she felt that we were obnoxious and were deliberately misbehaving. She often used competition as a way to get us to learn like the "normal students." Looking back on all of this, I see that this was all a cruel irony because she tried to get her students to become less angry, afraid and verbally and physically violent. Her anger got in the way all of the time. I can cite a few examples.

I took English One and I was the only seventh grader in the course among sixth-graders, which was embarrassing enough. But my teacher made things worse. In the beginning I noticed that she thought there was only one way of interpreting stories and poetry. I don't remember whose poetry we were discussing, but it was during the second week of classes. It was a Friday and we were walking to the McDonald's on San Pablo Avenue past Gilman Street. After a pleasant conversation she got really angry and nasty all of a sudden. All of the other students were already in the restaurant ordering their food. She told me I was "selfish" because I was only interested in my own poetry. That comment still makes me mad to this day. Here was an example of someone making an assumption, and as I said, assumptions are based on ignorance. That's when my anger with her began. During the three years I attended New Age she called me "selfish," "arrogant," "ignorant," a "martyr" and "prejudiced." I felt the same way about her. It seemed we were always angry at each other.

One time in history class during the spring of 1990 a group of boys made a joke, I forgot what about, but I laughed along with them. Angry, my teacher told me in a nasty tone of voice to "get out." I was so angry. I wondered why she didn't kick out the four boys who were disrupting the class more than me. I sat down across the hallway in the Grammar/ Vocabulary room.

Looking back on the web site I also noticed:

"We believe the genius in all children develops in environments where teachers understand, honor, and respect the learning process." (www. newageacademy.net.)

She respected some of the students' learning processes, but with me it was the complete opposite. Later on I began to figure out that she found me more obnoxious than she did most everyone else at the school. My tutor from ninth grade, Cecilia Caruso, said she felt the same way when I visited her in New York City this past October. There was always about two or three other students that she treated the same way she treated me. At least she didn't turn the entire school against me, like she did with at least one or two students each year. They were all white boys with some type of severe learning disability or emotional problem. She did put me in competition with one of the students who did the best at New Age. His name was Mark Goldman. At the time he was in sixth grade and had entered New Age on Halloween.

The class I did the worst in was Computers. The man who taught the class had a belligerent disposition. Once he told me, "If you don't do your homework for the next class I will jump down your throat!" He said this with a smile on his face and a vicious tone in his voice. He had little patience with children and no previous teaching experience. A year later, he enrolled in classes at the California Culinary Academy in San Francisco where he studied for a year and a half.

I unleashed my anger towards him by not doing the work in class and by not answering his questions. That made him angrier. He told me that he had to talk to my parents because I was "in serious trouble" in his class. I was getting a "D." I really didn't care. The following Monday he called up my mom and explained to her my behavior. She wasn't angry at me. I vented my anger towards my Computers teacher to Mom. I was close to tears. But she took my side over his. I don't really remember what happened after that, except I didn't interact with him any more.

Recently, Mom told me that she was surprised at how well I use electronics after I struggled in Computer Education at New Age Academy. My problems were mostly due to me feeling uncomfortable around my teacher, but also because the Apple computers weren't that good at the time. They were very difficult to use. The technology of Apple computers has dramatically improved over the last two decades.

I didn't really become comfortable with electronics until I bought my Compaq Presario PC in August of 1997. Now I own an Apple laptop, two Apple iPods: a Nano and a Shuffle, a Hewlett Packard digital camera, a Hewlett Packard printer, a Siemens T-Mobile cell phone, an iHome stereo for the iPod, and a Sony digital voice recorder. I found out about this tiny voice recorder while watching the movie *Nancy Drew*, starring Emma Roberts. Nancy Drew was holding a sleek white digital recorder that she was talking in to. Now I am very comfortable with electronics.

In middle school I blamed my problems on the computers rather than on my teacher. I wouldn't go near an Apple computer for many years. This was often my reaction when I struggled in something. For years I didn't take swimming classes because I didn't have good teachers and after I transferred from community college to U.C. Berkeley, I decided not to take any more English or Math classes because throughout my schooling I didn't have English and Math teachers that taught me in the way that I needed to be taught. (I luckily got a math waiver when I transferred, which was very hard to get.)

There were other hostile teachers at New Age. One of them taught Logic and Reasoning. Since I struggled in Logic and Reasoning, the fact that I had a young and inexperienced teacher who laughed at people when they didn't know something and who liked to yell a lot, did not help whatsoever. I didn't like her. I was always angry with her, which affected my performance in class. I held my anger in, which caused headaches and stomachaches like in Computer class. I punished her by again not doing the work and not paying attention in class. I don't really remember what we did in class. I didn't care if I made her angry. One time she kicked me out of class after yelling at me because Melinda and I got into an argument. Everyone was surprised because I usually was quiet in class. The teacher was angry and I didn't care. She gave us a lecture about getting along. It didn't work because I didn't like Melinda and she didn't like me.

The Grammar and Vocabulary teacher also got angry easily. She was the daughter of one of the other teachers and she also liked to yell a lot. Her temper got worse after she severely hurt her foot. She seemed to lose her temper over every little thing. One time she got nasty with me when I got angry with another student in class. I got angry back, but I held in my anger again. Once I heard her yelling at a kid in the principal's office. The kid was crying.

The lowest of the low was when the principal brought in this really angry guy to teach us a song that we were going to sing at commencement exercises. I was already upset because I found out at the last minute that for the next two Fridays I wasn't going to go to cartooning class. He was the angriest person I have ever seen in my life and I have seen a lot of angry people. I never saw him smile or talk in a calm, quiet voice. He was on his way to a heart attack or stroke. He sounded like a mentally ill person off of his medications. He talked to us in a demeaning and disrespectful way. He had one kid crying, I don't remember why, but this guy pulled three sixth graders, Doug, Jim M, and Danny and Doug's eighth grade brother, Robert aside. I didn't get along with any of them, so for a minute I was glad that they were getting yelled at but the man didn't give them constructive criticism. He started threatening them physically, saying he was going to beat them up. The principal was in the next room and didn't intervene. The commencement song was called "Doin' It Up." It was a mixture of jazz and R&B. I remember how unhappy I was singing it. Actually, none of us were happy singing it. I remember how bad we sounded when we sang. I don't know if the parents noticed how we felt. I think I was also angry about the "C" I received on my final project in Math when I felt I deserved an "A" because I worked harder on that project than I did on my English and Science final projects. I got an "A" on both of them. That was the first "A" I got in English.

For academic courses I took English, Math, Communications, Spanish, and Grammar and Vocabulary every morning. History and Geography were on Tuesday and Thursday afternoons and the entire school took these courses together. Science and Computer Education were on Monday and Wednesday afternoons. The girls took Health on Tuesday afternoons and the boys took Health on Thursday afternoons.

On Fridays we took elective courses. In the morning we did Homeroom where we dropped off our Thursday night homework. Then we took Sewing and then Drama. After lunch some of the students took Fine Art, some Cartooning and some Apprentice. I didn't like Sewing and Perceptual Skills because I struggled in both courses. I also felt really shy in Drama class. I didn't feel that way in The Children's Troupe. I think I was shy at New Age because I had to perform in front of my peers and I was worried that I would be laughed at.

For Physical Education courses we took Aikido on Wednesday afternoons, Yoga for the boys on Tuesday afternoons and for the girls on Thursday afternoons, and on Monday afternoons we took Gymnastics. I have never liked team sports since I don't like competition, so these P.E. courses were good for me emotionally. However, I think that those sports were the most likely cause of the serious back condition I have now. My spine doctor told me that the pre-teen and teenage years are when young women are most likely to get stress fractures or defects of the Pars Interarticularis of a vertebra. Also, the fractures or defects can weaken the bone so much that one of the vertebra slips over another, causing Spondylolisthesis, another condition I have. Bulging and herniated discs in and around the affected area, osteoarthritis (spondylosis) in and around the affected area, sciatica and cramping hamstrings are part of the condition. Some people get symptoms right away. Others, like me, don't have symptoms for many years after the slippage occurs. Some never get symptoms. The condition has caused my spine to sway, my torso to look shorter and bigger than it is really, and my pelvis to sway. According to my physical therapist, since I am super flexible, I could get injured more easily because my P.E. teachers pushed me harder than they did my classmates. I am very flexible because of the way my joints are designed and I have a sixth lumbar vertebra. My physical therapist said P.E. instructors are not trained to work with super flexible people. I can tell that my spine, hips, knees and ankles are also designed differently than most people's.

After going to multiple doctors over this condition for over two years, I now believe I shouldn't have been doing gymnastics, aikido and yoga. My spinal condition is genetic. Unfortunately, there were no other choices for P.E. In a perfect world I would have had the option of swimming, walking or low-impact aerobics (aerobics without running or jumping). What I really needed was a low-impact core-strengthening program. My core was never strong. But the principal's attitude seemed to be that what worked for her worked for everyone, and she encouraged her staff to think the same way. Now that I am adult I have a choice on what exercises I do.

I have been tested and treated for this condition since the holiday season of 2006. They did an X-ray, an MRI and an EMG (Electromyography) for testing my bones, discs and nerves. For treatment they put me on three potent oral painkillers to help the symptoms I have like stiffness, spasms, burning, tingling, numbness, cramping, dullness, aches and stabbing. I have also done physical therapy, ice and heat therapy, acupuncture, epidural steroid injections and a facet block. I don't know if any of the other students had stress fractures because there has never been a reunion and never will be one. I haven't talked to most of them in more than fifteen years. The doctors really don't know what to do because the problem is so complex. The spinal problems might be the cause of the neuropathy, but this is just a theory. The neurologist, after doing a few tests, did not know the cause.

I had some very positive experiences at New Age. Sometimes we took field trips on BART and/or MUNI. We went to the old De Young

Museum in San Francisco that was torn down on December 31, 2000 and reopened as a brand new structure on October 15, 2005. It was much smaller than the new one and the Asian Art Museum was only one room inside the De Young. The Asian Art Museum now stands in the Civic Center where the old main library used to be across the plaza from City Hall. It was where the old library used to be and before that the City Hall that was completely destroyed in the 1906 earthquake. The De Young Museum is still at the same site at Golden Gate Park. At the De Young we saw paintings by a fourteen-year-old Chinese artist named Yani Wang. She painted a lot of monkeys. Monkeys were her obsession. I haven't heard about any artwork from her since then. She is almost thirty-three now. We also went to see *Les Miserables* by Victor Hugo at the Curran Theatre, which didn't impress me. I only remember the turntable on the stage.

When I was a teenager, I had a hard time in "The Children's Troupe" as well. Before, I got along with everyone and I felt confident on stage. But starting in seventh grade things changed. I felt embarrassed that every time I put on the stage make-up my skin broke out. When I had my period, I felt embarrassed about accidents happening on stage. I felt the costumes cramped my style, especially the Converse sneakers. They were neither comfortable, nor cute. Mom and Jody thought they were.

I didn't get along with most of the members of The Children's Troupe. Niecy was one of them. Niecy joined the troupe when we were in fifth grade and we performed *joE*. *joE* was a musical whose text was built upon the many sayings and meanings of the word "joe," which was once synonymous with the words "clown" or "joke." Mom and Jody, in their book *Live on Stage!* talked about how we kids collaborated with them and the composer Ed Bogas. I remember on-going chases in and out of the wings, accompanied by a litany of historical kings and politicians named Joe, and a mock trial of an imaginary Joe, in which I was part of the jury. We performed *joE* again at the Florence Schwimley Little Theatre. One of my lines was "Life is always best when you're in the majority."

Anyway, Niecy and I fought on a constant basis during the 1989–1990 year. I remember her bad mouthing me to two girls in The Children's

Troupe during a dress rehearsal and they laughed at me. Their names were Sarah and Marlena. Marlena's mom was my science teacher at John Muir. I remember wanting to haul Niecy and these two girls backstage to smack them. What we fought over was so stupid that I don't remember. Niecy and I began to lose our strong friendship that year.

Dani was the nastiest member of The Children's Troupe. It is fair to say she was often out of control. Mom said that she was sometimes pleasant. I never saw the pleasant side of her. Dani told everyone, including the deaf children who I was friends with during the John Muir days, that I cussed all of the time. Three of the deaf girls, Bekah, Erica G and Erin got angry with me while Dani laughed. This incident happened in the spring of 1991 before the performance of *Handtalk*, a play based off of the book *Handtalk Happy Birthday* by Remy Charlip, Mary Beth and George Ancona. During the performance Bekah, who was seven, got up in my face making angry faces. Dani was laughing. I wanted to hit Dani, but this wasn't the time or the place. In the dressing room Dani and I got into a shoving match in front of Eva who was six and a half. Everyone was watching in shock, including Eva.

In 1992, when we arrived at the Laney College Theater for a performance of *Face the Music*, her father, who was Argentinean, had just destroyed the set of a play that was produced by the drama department at Laney College. This was because they hadn't cleaned off the set after their performance in time so that the stage would be ready for us to perform on. A letter, describing the incident, was sent from the Laney College Drama Department to Jody, Mom and The Children's Troupe members explaining his hissy fit. Dani was no longer there, which made the atmosphere at The Children's Troupe a whole lot better. The deaf kids seemed to have forgotten the incident the year before during *Handtalk*. I hadn't forgotten it and I still felt uncomfortable around the deaf kids.

Not only did the girls in The Children's Troupe damage my relationship with Niecy by trying to compete for Niecy's friendship, the girls across the street did as well. I must admit that ever since they moved into the neighborhood Niecy's attitude changed towards me for the worse. They threw rocks at my window one evening. Niecy and I began to fight in fifth and sixth grades, but not as much as we did in seventh grade.

One day, not far after the Loma Prieta Earthquake, she told me that we weren't "best friends in the whole wide world" anymore. We had been calling each other this since we were six or seven. I was so hurt that I felt off-guard. I literally did not know what to say. I don't remember what happened after that because the hurt turned into anger. I was so angry that I couldn't cry. When I get angry I black out, so I can't remember what happened.

From then on, when we invited her to places, she always asked if Rakia would come along. Rakia was one of the girls who lived across the street. I remember Mom explaining to her on the phone after telling Niecy, "no," that I always complained that when Rakia was around they would exclude me from conversations. Niecy came with us, much to her dismay. I could tell she was angry that we said "no" about Rakia coming.

I will admit that she did make sure to get together with me every once in a while and she did come to the school dance later on in the year. But we didn't interact with each other as much as we used to. When we were in tenth grade she moved out of the neighborhood to east Oakland because her mother didn't want her around the kidnapping suspect. Then the summer we were going to eleventh grade she moved to Atlanta. We have only interacted once in the last fifteen years but she still considers me her good friend, and I hers. I was angry often that year with Heather and Subira, but we got over our anger with time and I consider them my very good friends as well.

We listened to music, talked, laughed and read books. She came over to celebrate my thirteenth and fourteenth birthdays. She came with me to the semi-formal dance in May of 1990 that New Age Academy held. In 2007 Niecy came to visit us. We had a joyful reunion where we laughed a lot. She has two daughters, ages twelve and ten and she worked in promotions on behalf of Too Short, the hip-hop star. My dad is always praising her mother, Candice. She raised three kids herself, all of them achievers. Dad, Niecy and I sang on *Conjure*, a CD where singers like Taj Mahal and musicians like David Murray set my dad's songs to music. Niecy and I joined Dad in singing Cab Calloway's "Minnie the Moocher," which I have on my iPod since "Conjure" is on iTunes. While touring

Japan, Cab Calloway had collapsed about the same time as the recording. Dad said it was probably because he heard us sing.

I didn't miss seventh grade when it came to a close. I wrote a poem of appreciation to New Age Academy called "School Museum" that is in my book *Electric Chocolate*, emphasizing the positive experiences I had there.

SCHOOL MUSEUM

The dictionary says
that a museum is a building
full of interesting objects.
My school is a museum.

My school looks like
a tropical island
made of plywood
cactus plants and palm trees.

On each room divider
there are palm trees
just like the ones
in my backyard.
Of course, these are plywood
palm trees.

Four cactus plants live
on the walls
of the big room.

Real live banana trees
sit by hot spring water
and two others live
in the big room.

On a white pedestal
a green square rock
hides purple crystals
like a banker hoards
precious gems
in a safe place.

A clear globe
glitters purple, pink and blue
intersecting rays.
When you turn it on
it flashes neon.

There's a bamboo
waterfall that hits
ice crystal rocks
sunk into a pink tub.

And a rainbow colored
banner says:
"Let every day be
your masterpiece."

I worked with my teacher for two weeks in August of 1990 on math skills. She thought that I needed work on math because I was struggling. I remember being nasty towards her that summer. My anger was based on frustration and fear. One morning I showed my vulnerability and I started crying. I forget what exactly made me cry. I remember showing up to my summer sports camp at Cal still sniffling and having red eyes. I don't think my gymnastics classmates noted, but I needed the exercise to get out of my funk. I felt better as the morning went on. It was a wasted two weeks because my Math skills didn't improve. I felt angry not only because I was struggling but because it was summer vacation and I needed a vacation from English and math.

During July of 1990, when I was in Pittsburgh visiting my Grandma, *Electric Chocolate,* my second book of poetry was published by Raven's Bones Press in Alaska. When I entered eighth grade at the New Age Academy in the fall of 1990 the principal announced that it had been published. Right away I knew that I was going to have problems. The students got jealous and angry and they started making fun of me even though it was the first day of school. It was the same group of boys that gave me problems in the 1989–1990 school year. Doug and Danny no longer attended New Age Academy, but the other boys influenced this new kid named Zach to make fun of me. That lasted throughout the entire year.

A schoolmate named Noah, who was a seventh grader, lived in the Harz Mountains of the former West Germany from 1988–1990. He came back not that long before school started. The principal was talking to someone who was either from Germany or who had lived in Germany and she introduced Noah to her. That was the only part of the conversation that I caught. That was on the first day of school.

We concentrated on Germany a lot that fall because it was reunified on October 3, 1990. A month later we traveled to the old MoMA where we saw the "Degenerate Art," or in German "*Entartete Kunst*" exhibit. The years 1927–1937 were critical for artists in Germany. In 1927, the National Socialist Society for German Culture was formed. The aim of this organization was to halt the "corruption of art" and inform the people about the relationship between race and art. By 1933, the terms "Jewish," "Degenerate," and "Bolshevik" were in common use to describe almost all modern art. In 1937, Nazi officials purged German museums of works the Party considered to be degenerate. From the thousands of works removed, 650 were chosen for a special exhibit of Entartete Kunst. The exhibit opened in Munich and then traveled to eleven other cities in Germany and Austria. In each installation, the works were poorly hung and surrounded by graffiti and hand written labels mocking the artists and their creations. Over three million visitors attended making it a "blockbuster" exhibition. One painting we saw showed Joseph and Mary as Latin Americans with black hair, brown eyes and olive skin. I saw that same exhibit at the Altes Museum on the Museum Island of Berlin a year and a half later.

I didn't pay attention to Noah for about a month after the school year started. I forgot how we met but we talked about traveling a lot. He traveled around Europe to places like England, the Netherlands, Belgium, France, Switzerland, Italy, Denmark and what was then called Czechoslovakia. I hadn't really paid attention to Europe that much until then. I started talking about wanting to travel there. I had only been to

England at the time. A year and a half later it was time for me to visit Germany and a little bit of France and Switzerland. Then in 1993 I went to the Netherlands and in 1994 I traveled to Germany again.

Meeting Noah was when I started bragging about my travels. People didn't like it when I bragged. I often talked about my travels at inappropriate times. It took me quite a few years to figure out that bragging on myself turned people off. I still do it sometimes. When people brag it turns me off, too. I found it inappropriate when I was in graduate school and the women would show off their wedding rings. There are a group of upper class middle-aged white women at the Y who brag about places they go to and material things while changing clothes in the locker room and I don't find it appropriate. I often think about Noah and my schoolmates at New Age not liking me for bragging when I see this behavior. Mom told me that they need to learn from their mistakes on their own like I did. Dad tells me, "People are going to hate you if you brag." Hate is a strong word, so I know he really means they will get jealous and angry.

There were two things I learned that year. I did have a crush on Noah and I learned that coming on too strong and too fast was something people didn't like. When I left New Age in 1992, his mother, Mary, told Mom that Noah wasn't into girls yet. I lost a few "friendships" because I came on too strong and too fast. In return, I didn't like the unpredictable behavior of my classmates. I also didn't like people who were two-faced. I still don't like people like that. I like people to be honest with me from the beginning about how they feel about me so I know whether I should stay away or not. My schoolmates were definitely unpredictable. It was difficult making friendships and being professional with them.

I remember one thing a seventh-grade girl said that really hurt me at the time. This girl came to New Age in November of 1989. She and I got along very well the previous year. However, she started the 1990–1991 school year mean. She had changed for the worse over the summer it seemed to me. She got even meaner around the time her mother was diagnosed with cancer in October of 1990 and the meanness got worse as the year went on. I didn't know at the time her mother had cancer. Her mother was also an alcoholic. According to the way this girl would describe her relationship with her mother to her friends, her mother was a mean drunk. I think she drank and drove as well. Mom smelled alcohol on her breath one afternoon. I vaguely remember this girl crying and going to talk in private to Carrie, a ninth-grader that I had a huge fight with a couple of weeks later and after that we only spoke to each other out of anger. She and I began to fight a lot. Our friendship was damaged beyond repair and it really hurt. One day, our teacher left the health class for a minute for some reason and this girl started going though the teacher's book bag. I told her not to go through Mrs. Cooper's things. She replied, "Fuck you, Tennessee!" I was so angry that I wanted to hit her. It was on my fourteenth birthday when that incident happened, February 28, 1991. Seventeen years later, that spat seems trivial. Now that I look back on it, her disrespect was not personal. Her mother died in 1995 or 1996, and so her behavior might have been traceable to depression.

I also remember two students who came in the spring semester of 1991 who I also thought were going to be good friends. They were named Antony and Rowena. It turned out to be not the case. Heather and the girl I mention above turned Rowena against me with their behaviors, and Jim B. and Zach turned Antony against me. Two other girls spread a rumor around New Age that I was a lesbian and that I was a "ho." They were always in my business. They were black girls who perpetuated the stereotype of the loud and angry black woman. I could tell that they were racist towards white people by the comments they made. One of them made a crack to me about my mother being Jewish. I never saw that girl interact with any of the white or biracial students, though she was friends with Carrie. She was okay with Carrie being biracial. To this day I don't understand that logic. Maybe it is because racists make exceptions for those others whom they like.

Melinda did interact with both white people and black people and Carrie, yet she was nasty towards me. One time she got really nasty with me in Communications class in my ninth-grade year. During an assignment about bragging that we had in our Communications class, another boy joined her in her nastiness. The teacher did nothing to intervene. She told our teacher, "Tennessee always brags." I got really angry and said that I wasn't going to read my assignment out loud because of her "bitchy like" behavior. They both said, "You should give her an 'F', Bill," to our teacher. I wanted to reach across the table and smack them both, but I held my anger in. Later on I vented to my tutor, Cecilia Caruso, when we were discussing the assignment. Melinda was really sweet with everyone else, but with me she was nasty. I had a strong dislike towards her. Being multiracial makes me understand through experience that there is racism among every race. Those in the majority merely have more power to enforce it, or pass laws reflecting their bigotry.

A lot of the students had emotional problems. Some were also going to New Age because they were having a hard time in the public schools, just like me. There were a lot of verbal and physical incidents. I would say that about 95 per cent of the students had emotional problems along with being a teenager. Some had a parent with an illness. Others were dealing with a new stepparent, a parent who neglected them, drugs and other problems I didn't know about. The media image of the dysfunctional family is black; many of these kids are white.

Most of them did a lot of trivial teasing, but some were abusive. Some of the boys rubbed me the wrong way because they showed me in a weird way they liked me. It was harassment to me. There was one boy that was angry and abusive. None of the teachers did anything about him. He hit me over the head one time with a dictionary.

Eighth grade was almost as bad as seventh grade. I was put back into English One for the first two weeks of school even though I had published a book that was praised by famous authors. That only lasted for two weeks because I went home and complained to my parents. Dad wrote a letter to the principal. Much to her disapproval I was soon put into English Two. I don't know what he said to her because I didn't see the letter.

I remember that in October of 1990, we were assigned to make something or other that required mechanical skills in our General Science class. I'm not good at building things so I decided not to do the assignment. Nobody did the project except for Mark and Noah. Mark bragged about his project. Noah also did the assignment because he was known around the school as "the architect." He had a talent for architecture and he was really good with his hands. Unfortunately, Noah's assignment was destroyed because three boys were "play fighting" and they accidentally knocked it over. Noah was so upset that he was crying. That happened the morning of the due date. I remember that was the day that Germany reunited.

After a conference between myself, Mom and my teacher, I wrote a paper instead of doing the original project. I got a "B-." I was upset because I thought I deserved an "A." To this day I still don't know how I could have handled that because I am not good at putting things together, with or without instructions. Now that I am thirty-one instead of thirteen, I understand that the teachers have to cater to all of their students' learning styles. What the teacher should have done was given me an alternative assignment. The school was supposed to do that according to the guidelines of the Americans with Disabilities Act. Since they didn't believe in learning disabilities, that wasn't going to happen. That was my lowest point that year.

In the spring semester my grades improved dramatically. I did much better in English, Math, Vocabulary and Grammar. I always did well in Science, Health, P.E. and History. History and Science have always been my best subjects. Computer Education and Spanish were still the same. I had a Spanish teacher from a French-speaking country who was just learning Spanish herself.

One of my teacher's there didn't believe that racism existed. She often said, "Racism is in your head." Sometimes, unwittingly, she made racist comments herself. When this teacher said the word "mulatto" one time in History I told her to say "biracial" instead of "mulatto." I told her that the word was derogatory. She told me that the word was only derogatory to me. Often she would tell us that when her mother pulled her hair so tight, her eyes would slant like an Asian's. She would even pull her eyes back into a slant. Maybe she thought this was a funny story.

One afternoon in History class Jordan called my nose "a big honk." I found out that he is a descendant of writer Jean Toomer, who was mixed with many nationalities like German, English, Dutch, Jewish and African-American. I got really angry and nasty with him because I take racism very seriously. This was the only class where the entire school got together outside of homeroom. We were planning for our trip to Arizona and we were going to look up the places in the red atlas we were going to visit.

The teacher called Jordan and me to the front of the room to where she stood in front of the black podium. It felt like a judge calling two lawyers to the bench like I see in the court shows I watch. She got angry with me instead of with Jordan. I forgot what she said word for word, but I know she said some nasty things to me. Usually when she was angry with me she would verbally abuse me or roll her eyes. That day there was physical abuse. She told Jordan to hit me. He hit me on the left shoulder hard enough to cause a bruise. After that happened, this teacher wanted me to thank Jordan for hitting me. When I refused she got livid and threatened to suspend me. I had to apologize. She told me that Jordan hitting me would maybe teach me to learn how to respect her and the other students and I deserved it because I was obnoxious. To this day this incident still makes me very angry even though she was the one with the problem. This incident makes me want to cry. I also get sick to my stomach. Now I realize that it was partly my fault for letting Jordan and the teacher walk all over me, because I did not tell my parents about it nor did I say anything in response to stop the behavior.

This teacher would also make remarks or do things that some would consider sexist. She told us girls in our health class that if we wanted to have both a boy and a girl that we should have a girl first and then a boy, since a little boy would be violent towards their baby sister. I felt that it was odd not only because we couldn't control that (since biology says that the father is the one that determines the sex of the baby by producing an X or a Y chromosome) and also because it was discriminatory towards boys. Then the girls started repeating this. I was the only girl smart enough not to have the teacher influence how I thought.

One day two teachers started talking about the difference between white boys and black boys. A young biracial boy, named Antony, became so angry that he had to leave the room. His teacher didn't understand why he got so angry. I forget exactly what she said, but it was pretty bad. But she was totally unaware of what she said to make him angry. Some of my feminist university professors shared these attitudes. They'd select only black women for their reading lists. In one class the fiction chosen was so biased against black men that some of the black men enrolled in the class dropped out of it.

Our History teacher was very closed-minded. She mostly talked about Europe and the Renaissance. The year before, I remember a black boy complaining about this. She taught us a lot of Native American history but she didn't teach enough African-American, Latino/Chicano-American, and Asian-American history. We were discussing Columbus's arrival in America. She started talking about Italians. She still thinks that Columbus "discovered" America. She said that the reason northern Italians have gray eyes and red hair or blue eyes and blonde hair is because the sun barely comes out in that part of Italy. She said that the reason that southern Italians have dark brown eyes and black hair is because they are in the sun a lot more. That is not true. The reason that southern Italians are dark skinned is because they have an African heritage. The Moors came from North Africa and occupied large parts of Italy for 300 years. Throughout my education I've heard teachers make ignorant remarks like this. For an extremely smart woman she sounded stupid sometimes.

She only had us read European stories in English as well. She was really into the classics and she also loved classical music. I found that boring after a while. I wanted to read more modern stories and poems by writers of other ethnic groups. I also wanted to listen to different music.

I would say that even though she couldn't get along with me because of my different learning style, she was a dedicated teacher. I came to this conclusion because of an incident that took place during in the fall of 1990. It was during History class and a majority of the class, including me, wasn't prepared. I forgot what the assignment was. She gave us a lecture and then, suddenly she threw chalk. It hit the ground and bounced up into the homework basket. She began to cry and fled the room. She told me years later that the reason she was so angry was because society taught us that it was okay for us to come unprepared. As I wrote in my poem, there were some memorable and wonderful experiences to be had at the New Age Academy as well.

Between May 11 and May 17, 1991, New Age Academy traveled by bus to Arizona. We visited Kingman, Flagstaff, First Mesa, Second Mesa, Canyon de Chelly on the Navajo Reservation, the Painted Desert and the Grand Canyon. We drove through Death Valley and the Mohave Desert to get there. I remember how inspiring that trip was. One really great experience was when Noah's father Lee brought his telescope with him. In the dark desert near the Hopi Cultural Center on Second Mesa, we were able to see Jupiter because the sky was so clear. I was the only one who took advantage of the situation.

Soon after coming back from Arizona, I graduated eighth grade with higher grades then I started with. I got my diploma and a yellow belt in Aikido.

I started my last year at New Age Academy for ninth grade in the fall of 1991. I had changed a lot over the summer. I started to stick up for myself and not care about whether I hurt or angered the people whose behaviors offended me. My acne had cleared up a lot even though I stopped taking the medication because I had some harsh side effects from it. My hair got a little longer. I wasn't as insecure.

Mom didn't want to enroll me at Arrowsmith because she wasn't sure that it was going to stay open. I didn't know that until quite recently. She didn't know what other school I could go to so I returned to New Age. There weren't a lot of options of high schools for me to go to.

On the second day of my summer break between eighth and ninth grade, I went with Mom to New Age to discuss this with the principal. She asked me if I wanted to go there another year. I should have said "no" instead of "yes." My parents realize now that they made a mistake in sending me back there another year. Mom told me if she knew about the teacher telling Jordan to hit me she would have pulled me out of New Age that day and taken me to Arrowsmith.

Even though I didn't have nearly as many problems as I had in eighth and seventh grade there were still a lot of problems. The fall of 1991 started off shaky. For one, I was the oldest and I felt awkward and out of place. I entered the building on the first day of school already knowing that I had made a mistake coming there another year. I had met a new girl named Nicole. I'm not sure what grade she was in. I didn't pick up the cues quickly enough to realize that she didn't want to be friends, because I was working too hard to build a friendship with her. When I finally figured out she didn't want the friendship I moved on by simply not interacting with her, which is what I do when I realize someone doesn't want the kind of friendship I want. That way I won't be hurt.

The principal made up two phrases. One was, "If you make the same mistake over and over you are stupid." The other phrase was, "A lesson repeats itself until it is learned." Since I struggled in Math, Communications, Logic and Reasoning, English and Computers, these are the expressions she'd batter me with because I was slower than most of the class. That got old after the second time. I would tell people to "shut up" in a nasty tone every time they said that, regardless of whether or not they were teachers or classmates. I don't think the school administration was really aware of the deep impact these phrases had on the students.

I began to become more jealous of Mark that year. One morning my teacher got really angry with me. She was almost as angry with me as she was the day she asked Jordan to hit me. I think I was interrupting her to ask a question but there was still no excuse for her telling me to "shut up" in front of my peers and then rolling her eyes and laughing. Then she told me that she would "scream" if I didn't behave the way she wanted me to. I decided to get nasty with her. I called her a "bitch" and Mark an "asshole" not caring if they heard. Then I told her that "she acted like a teenager" and she was "a mean and angry individual who needed professional help." She and Mark were in so much shock that they didn't say anything. The rest of the class was shocked that I had finally showed some backbone. I noticed that I got a little more respect from my classmates that year.

The teachers often played favorites. The kids who had an intelligence that matched hers, i.e., sitting still, being good at everything, and getting good grades, were always treated with respect. Josh was very cool about his success at New Age. I liked Josh a lot. We got along very well. But Mark always bragged. Every day the teacher would let him stand in front of her podium and call out the answers to our Algebra homework. They were like partners in crime.

My grades got much better. I got all "As" and "Bs" and during the first grading period I got the highest grades in the school. Mark was jealous and angry. It was great to see him that way. He was so mad he wouldn't look at me or talk to me for the six weeks in between the report cards. I was happy. I had wanted him to shut up and sit down for a long time.

We had a new and better Spanish teacher and a new and better computer teacher during the 1991–1992 school year. Our Spanish teacher was from Colombia and her name was Esperanza. I struggled with Spanish both in middle school and high school. German is my language. It was much easier for me to conjugate verbs in German. German is quite similar to English. During my second trip to Germany I spoke a lot of German. In Computer class we had a teacher named Patricia. She was very patient and she helped us figure out how to do our homework. I enjoyed her very much and my grades went from "Ds" to "Bs." We were all glad she was teaching.

Things changed for the better in The Children's Troupe as well. There was a smaller crowd, which was much better. The girls who gave me problems were no longer there and I was at a better emotional place. We all wrote a rap song in eight languages. It was called "We're Ready." The languages were: English, Spanish, French, Italian, German, Japanese, Chinese and Yoruba. I got to speak in German, Yoruba and French. Even though we were speaking in foreign languages the year before in *Handtalk* it didn't seem all that hard to me. We also sang a group song, "We are the Future" while we danced and did sign language. We all got to wear our own clothes as long as they were brightly colored. We had to wear the Converse sneakers. I wore a turquoise sweatshirt, a purple shirtsleeve tee, turquoise biking shorts by Express, magenta DKNY tights, purple socks and my Converse high-tops. I had a big multi-colored bow in my hair.

Two of my poems premiered on our March 28, 1992 performance at the Laney College. One was called "Three Heavens and Hells." It was a twenty-minute piece originally composed by Meredith Monk, my mother's friend from Sarah Lawrence College, who is a dancer, choreographer, composer and musician. Ms. Monk sang this song with Allison Easter, Dina Emerson and Kate Geissinger. It is one of the tracks on Monk's CD *Volcano Songs*. The CD can be bought on iTunes.com.

> There are three heavens and hells
> People   Animal   Things
> heaven and   heaven and   heaven and
> hell   hell   hell

During *Face the Music* the Oakland Children's Chorus sang "Three Heavens and Hells." The poem was published in *Electric Chocolate*. We got to do a shadow puppet performance followed by an introduction by the deaf kids: Bekah, Jane, Andy, Lidia, the two Erica's and Erin. It was really cool because I had enjoyed looking at shadows since I was a little kid. In the piece I was the lion whose home was being encroached on by a bulldozer. "Three Heavens and Hells" came in five pieces: the Introduction, People Heaven and Hell, Animal Heaven and Hell, Things Heaven and Hell and then the Conclusion.

After "Three Heavens and Hells" premiered in *Face the Music* I traveled to New York in December of 1993 and took a bow while Meredith Monk performed "Three Heavens and Hells" at Merkin Hall. In October of 1994 Meredith Monk toured Europe and performed "Three Heavens and Hells" in Cologne, Germany. She wanted me to come to Cologne, but I was in Frankfurt at another event and couldn't make it. In June of 1998 Meredith Monk came out to San Francisco and performed "Three Heavens and Hells" at Davies Symphony Hall during the American Mavericks Performance Series directed by Michael Tilson Thomas. In 2007 Meredith Monk performed "Three Heavens and Hells" in New York with a children's choir.

My other poem, "The Old Parents Blues," music composed by musician Carman Moore, was performed. The poem was published in *Airborne.*

THE OLD PARENTS BLUES

My parents took me to
the movies tonight.
You should have been there.
It was a sight.

It was so funny I cracked up
but then I got the blues.
It was so funny I cracked up
but then I got the blues.

Oh, my father forgot
the cinema number.
We had to go back again
and ask the usher.

It was so funny I cracked up
but then I got the blues.
It was so funny I cracked up
but then I got the blues.

When we came home
my mom didn't know
she'd kept her sunglasses on
all through the show.

My mom said, "Did the lights go out?"
she took off her glasses
with a hoot and a shout.
Dad said, "I wondered what that was all about."

That's why I'm singing this song.
Oh, we were cracking up a storm.
But then I got the blues.
But then I got the blues.

Tell me what's next
as they go into the night.
Will they cross the street
with a Seeing Eye dog
on a red light?

Will they lose the car
forgetting where it's parked?

When they speak will their words
be off the mark?

But mostly I'm worried
things going as I can
that maybe
they will forget
who I am.

So that's why I'm singing this song.
Oh, we were cracking up a storm.
But then I got the blues.
But then I got the blues.

In the performance we made a car using four people and we wore papier-mâché masks that were molded by a young woman a few weeks before. It was a great way for my poetry to be advertised and for The Children's Troupe to end.

One day I had my last straw at New Age. Instead of our vocabulary lesson the ninth graders had before school, the teacher excused Melinda and Rowena, and I got to air my grievances. She had sensed that I was quite angry for a long time. The first thing I said was that I had been irritated with her two favorite phrases. Then I told her that I didn't like the way she had been treating me in the past three years and the name-calling that she used. (Now I know that she thought that she was trying to help me instead of hurt me by name-calling. She was trying to motivate me to learn the way she wanted me to learn.) I also told her I was still angry with her for asking Jordan to hit me and then telling me to thank him for that and I would never forgive her for that. I told her that I didn't like the fact that she instructed the students to critique my behavior because I didn't pay them to give me an education and I already had a therapist at Kaiser. I also told her I didn't like the fact that she told the students my grades because it was none of their business. And I didn't like her humiliating me in front of my peers because I didn't answer the English and Math questions the way she wanted me to and that there are no right or wrong answers to interpreting a poem or a story. I also asked her how she could call me "prejudiced" and a "martyr," when she made racist, sexist, and anti-disabled comments, and when she fabricated incidents between us to my parents.

She decided to make my grievances the topic of our homeroom discussion. I could tell that she was very upset. She told the school, "Someone told me that I humiliate students in this school." I remember Antony responding by saying that the word "humiliate" was a bit harsh but he agreed that he didn't want his grades known and that she had a tendency to put down students in front of their peers. The school all agreed except for Mark. That was no surprise. She was often very angry when a student disagreed with her teaching methods. One time when I was in seventh grade an eighth-grade boy said that her teaching methods were like those of a "Nazi." He had some severe learning disability or ADHD. It was obvious that she had gotten away with her behaviors for the past ten years. There was little supervision at this school, so she hardly received any criticism of her teaching methods.

In frustration, the teacher met with my mother and me after school that day. She told me that she didn't know how my brain worked after two and a half years of working with me. I didn't know how to respond to this or what to think about that comment. To this day I can't interpret that comment but what I think she was trying to say was that my intelligence didn't match the intelligence that she was used to working with. I also think she meant she couldn't understand my social and academic difficulties. I don't understand them myself.

After wanting to go to Germany for a year and a half I finally went from May 19–June 1, 1992. I took Delta, Swissair (now called Swiss) and Lufthansa. We flew into Basel and then drove a little bit through France to Freiberg. On that trip I traveled to Freiberg, Frankfurt, Berlin, Potsdam, Nuremberg and Erlangen. I read from my poetry in Potsdam in the former East Germany. It is southwest of Berlin. We went through the old Checkpoint Charlie to get there. The school building where I read was originally the headquarters of the Stasi, the dreaded East German police, but because Germany had been recently reunified, and the Stasi no longer existed, it had been converted to a university.

On this trip to Germany I got to visit places like the Black Forest, the Naturmuseum Senckenberg (the Natural History Museum in Frankfurt) the Altes Museum on the Museum Island of Berlin and the Museum of Ethnography also in Berlin. In Frankfurt we stayed at the Hotel Diana on Westendstrasse. The room we stayed in was very mysterious and old fashioned. The room is hard to describe. My grandfather, Bennie S. Reed, had passed away a month before. He came to me in that room. I really enjoyed myself over there. I was unhappy about coming back because I had to deal with my New Age classmates and teachers, and I wasn't in the mood to deal with them.

There was another major problem in ninth grade. I was doing a final paper in my Grammar class and I thought I did a good job. Dad did as well. The Grammar and Vocabulary teacher, scribbled all over my paper in a very hostile and argumentative way. She had graded it when I was in Germany. I went home in tears due to exhaustion, jetlag from my German travels, frustration and anger. My father told me to calm down so he assisted me with the paper. He called up the teacher, and when he asked what her background was, she hung up on him. The day I turned in the paper I complained to the principal who of course sided with the Grammar teacher. I've found this was a part of education; when you have a conflict with a teacher, other teachers, counselors, and administrators will always take the teacher's side.

Despite all of my problems at New Age, I did learn to organize my notes better. I also learned how to do basic research and how to make note cards for research papers. I liked the fact that the principal believed in teaching outside of the classroom. I enjoyed taking the BART rides to MoMA, to the De Young Museum, and the California Culinary Academy. I also liked going to the Ropes Course. Despite my conflicts with some of the students, Arizona was one of the most inspiring trips I have ever been on. I learned a lot of things about Native Americans that I would never learn in the classroom. I got to see the Hopi and Navajo reservations. I also liked the museum trips and the performances we went to see. The field trips were all I really liked about New Age.

When I look back at those years at New Age I've concluded that I did have a love/hate relationship with the principal. It might be a cliché and as simple as that. To this day I don't understand why. Maybe because she was tall and thin, had the hairstyle and skin tone that I wanted or maybe it was because she was an adult and she dressed well. Maybe it was because she had the career I wanted. On October 4, 2002 I finally cut off my relationship with her altogether when she told me I could eat lunch with her and the rest of the staff as long as I didn't "dominate the conversation." I had worked with her about six weeks in 2002 to get the skills I needed to teach. She said that she would always love me. That was our goodbye. New Age Academy closed at the end of the 2006–2007 school year due to financial difficulty and her health fading. She put her life into that school, suffered financial and enrollment setbacks, had to move from building to building in order to support her vision of what an education should be. And maybe years from now I'll make another assessment of whether she succeeded or failed.

CHAPTER SIX

Tenth Through Twelfth Grade

AFTER A LOT OF TRAVELING I ENTERED TENTH GRADE IN THE fall of 1992 at Arrowsmith Academy. It started off shaky. I had a cold and an ear infection, which I got flying to Seattle. My mom got seriously ill about the second day of classes and was admitted to the Emergency Room. She was near death. Kaiser didn't know the cause of her cramps and rapid weight loss. It was my Uncle, Michael LeNoir, a doctor, who knew that it was serious without even examining her. He just listened to her symptoms. He told her to go to the emergency room at once. He probably saved her life. They had to do surgery on her that evening and they didn't know what they were going to find. She had something called "Congenital Obstruction of the Bowels." Evidently she had some scar tissue since birth near the entrance to the large intestine that grew so big it closed up the entrance. She'd had a similar episode while living in New York as a young dancer. She was one of the original Judson Church avant-garde dancers, whose influence on modern dance was cutting edge.

Mom stayed in the hospital for eleven days. It was hard to see Mom in this condition. Dad and Jody took over her class at Arrowsmith. Dad said that after teaching her high school drama class, he felt like having a drink even though he hadn't had a drink in ten years.

Between September and November of 1992, Mom and I were both having a difficult time. I had to go to the ER myself because the reaction to the sulfa-based antibiotic I was taking for the ear infection was severe. I had a severe rash, a high fever that wouldn't come down and rapid breathing. I had some tests done and then I was given Amoxicillin and sent home. I found out later that sulfa-based antibiotics were not supposed to be for ear infections. The rash went away and the fever went down but I got a yeast infection and then had to go back to the doctor again. It was awful having that in class. I helped Mom lift things up and vacuum the house. We hired a housekeeper because Mom was too weak and I was to busy.

After this ordeal my eighteen-year-old cousin, Marquel, Uncle Michael's youngest daughter, was killed in an automobile accident near her school in Virginia. It was during her freshman year at Hampton University. It was such a shame because I knew that she was going to have a great future. She was an outstanding student in high school and she was beautiful. The funeral was held in Oakland at Saint Theresa's Church. I went through a long mourning period. While visiting New York in February of 1996, I lit a candle for her at Saint Patrick's Cathedral. I broke down and had to return to the hotel. Since her death I have visits from her in my dreams. I have to be really relaxed for this to happen. I also have dreams about Bennie S. Reed, my grandfather. I inherited this gift from my grandmother, Thelma Virginia Reed, who is psychic. She talks about these psychic experiences in her book *Black Girl from Tannery Flats*. This was the third death I experienced in 1992. My dear friend Paul Lofty died in February of that year. I also went through a period of anger at that time because of my illness, Mom's illness and Marquel's death. I often got nasty with some of my schoolmates.

I wasn't as close to Marquel as I was to my older cousins Monique, Mijnon and Michele. I remember Marquel as a shy and quiet child. She was smart and always talked to me. I remember her at my uncle's doctor office working on the computer and sharing jokes with the other receptionists and me. She wanted to become a Med. student, which is what she was hoping to study at Hampton. In the winter after finals, I was so exhausted from all of these ordeals that I caught a bad respiratory flu.

TODAY, SUNDAY

Today, Sunday,
the twenty-seventh
of December,
was supposed to
be Marquel's birthday.

The weather fit the day:
gray, gloomy, cold;
Marquel was supposed to
be nineteen.

She died November 6, 1992
in a car accident.
This was in Hampton, Virginia
where she was a freshman
pre-Med student in college.

There were five passengers in the car
when the driver fell asleep
and the car crashed into a tree.
The other four lived,
but Marquel died.

We can't say whose fault it was,
but the driver must feel
really scared and guilty.

I remember the day of the funeral.
We went into the Oakland hills
trying to find the Church.
Instead, we found burnt down houses.

When we found Lake Temescal
we knew we were going the right way.
The Church was so crowded
we had to stand up for a long time.

When her best friend spoke about her
and began to cry
I began to cry.

We got lost
two more times that day.
We went straight
from school to her house,
going down Thornhill
trying to find Mountain Boulevard
and going up and down up Snake Road
onto Manzanita Drive.

We watched *Cinderella*
with two kids,
Marquel's cousins,
named Brianna and Jordan.
I talked to them
and ate dinner.
Then we drove back home.

Now when I work
at my uncle's doctors office
she won't be there
typing on the computer
and talking on the phone.
It will be so weird.

At Arrowsmith, I did well in school and got on the honor roll. That is except for English. My teacher, Ms. Brooks, was very frustrated with me. She didn't really understand my style of writing. I didn't do so well on her tests. She had trouble with me because of my reading comprehension problem. But she didn't get angry or frustrated with me in front of the class. The frustration came out when she graded me with "Cs" in her class. I was frustrated because I didn't understand what she wanted me to do. I found out later she was racist towards the White students because she wanted to teach a course on slavery and said it would be for black students only. She was a drug addict.

I liked my History teacher, Ms. Bullen. She was the first history teacher whose view of History wasn't Eurocentric. She said that Christopher Columbus had made a mistake looking for India and went west instead of east. She also told us that the reason why Native Americans are called American Indians is because he thought he was in India. She said that he had a big role in the extermination of the Native Americans in the New World by bringing diseases from Europe. She also told us that he had died of Syphilis from raping Native women who were infected with it. They had caught it from one of his shipmates. She also was the first one who talked about the end of Apartheid in South Africa. When I was at New Age Nelson Mandela got out of jail.

I liked my Health teacher, Mrs. Barrow. She laughed a lot and made the class very interesting. I missed her when she left. She had injured her feet and the stairs were too much for her to take. She also taught me a lot and cheered me up. The second teacher who came in, whose name I forget, was a disappointment. I didn't care for her attitude a lot of the time. She seemed racist towards light-skinned and White people.

My Biology teacher Jenny Ruckleshaus, was also a favorite. She was a good teacher and made Biology interesting to me. We had weekly debates in class, which happened on Friday mornings. They were about many different topics. One was about Euthanasia. We were broken up into groups. We had oral quizzes instead of written quizzes before we moved onto the next subject. Our major project was to write a paper on a disease that we had or our family had. Mom said she didn't want me to talk about her operation so I talked about my chronic middle ear infections. I went to the health education department at Kaiser, which is in the basement of 3779 Howe Street. That used to be where I saw my pediatrician. All of the pediatrics used to be there, however the hematology/oncology department for children is still there, I think. The Podiatry department is where my pediatrician used to be. Now I use the library to buy equipment for my back.

The second semester of tenth grade was much better. I did better in terms of grades and I felt better about myself. I think that tenth grade was the best year in school that I had in terms of grades. I got all "As" and "Bs" both in fall and spring semesters despite all of the problems in my life that I experienced that year. But I had trouble with four girls who were in seventh grade. One in particular was Christine, who thought she was an expert on India because she had been there a few times, an attitude that I have no patience for.

I evidently had done something unforgivable during our women's studies class in the fall of 1992, not long after the semester had started. It was recently after Mom's surgery and I had also just gotten over the cold and ear infection. So I was already on edge. Christine got angry with me because she felt I was insulting her religion, which was Buddhism. I forgot what I had said, but I apologized to her and tried to move on but she wasn't willing to forgive me, so I got angry with her and said a few choice words. Therefore, we both made mistakes that we couldn't let go of.

Arrowsmith claimed itself as a multicultural school. The extent of its multiculturalism was a day of African-American, Latin American, Asian American, Native-American, women and gay/lesbian history. There was no disabled history day at all. The other one hundred and seventy-four days of school was straight White male history and literature. Christine said, "Why don't we have a European day?" I told her we study White history and literature all of the time, so every day is a European day. Then to add insult to injury I told her, "You are not an expert on India or Buddhism." She thought she knew everything. One time we almost got into a fist fight in art class over her know-it-all attitude. I probably would have won the fight since I was taller, slimmer and more in shape. She also insulted my friend, Alexis, whom I ran into again when she attended graduate school at Mills the same time I did. Christine and I never got over our differences. Just that statement about having a European day showed me that she lacked common sense.

There was also a young man named Ryan who came in the middle of the semester. He was in eleventh grade, but he looked much older. He was a nasty person. He called me "stupid" a lot. I don't know what his issue was. I don't remember what any of our conflicts were about, but our constant conflicts caused a rift between my friend David S and me. David S and I never had the friendship we had before Ryan came to Arrowsmith even after Ryan left. By the end of the year I was worn out. I needed a distance from my schoolmates.

After the school year let out we traveled to the Netherlands, visiting Amsterdam, The Hague and Eindhoven. That was enough of a distance for me. I got my wish and saw the Anne Frank House. Anne Frank meant a lot to me because she was a teenage fiction and journal writer, she was Jewish, she talked a lot like me, and she influenced my style of short story and journal writing. I remember learning about her in second grade. That's when I became interested in her life. Just as Anne Frank's diary has challenged the current attempt on the part of some to say that the Holocaust didn't happen, I hope that this book will challenge the myths that surround the teaching of the learning disabled. One of my prize possessions is a photo of me standing in front of Anne Frank's statue. I also got to take a ride on the Canal Bus where I rode on the Gentleman, Empress, and the Princess canals. The Anne Frank House is located on the Princess Canal.

We spent most of the trip in The Hague. In The Hague I saw the late Queen Juliana in the main square. It was beautiful between the old buildings, the cobblestone and the recessional. I also got to visit the Mauritshuis Museum, The Hague's famous art museum. We also took a tram to the North Sea. There was a beautiful sand castle. The sand castle image was of a Middle Eastern palace, statues that I see on building pediments, and temples. A pharaoh was imprinted in the sand. People bungee jumped off of a crane. Dad was wondering if we were going to see Norway and Sweden, but we couldn't.

I began eleventh grade in the fall of 1993. I worked very hard in Geometry more so than I did in my other subjects. Everyone says Geometry is very easy because it has to do with shapes and that my trouble with it is psychological. It isn't very easy for me. I went to a tutor. We tutored in Geometry mostly. I eventually got a "C" average in Geometry but I got "As" and "Bs" in my other courses. In the spring of 1994, after our late-January finals my teacher dropped me from Geometry. She wasn't a good teacher for me because she didn't know how to teach me. I took Physical Education earlier in the morning and Spanish right before lunch. For fourth period I did Study Hall.

I didn't like P.E. either except for basketball. It was always me and the guys when it came to basketball. The girls would play ping-pong, and Greta, who entered Arrowsmith during the second semester, had a sprained ankle so she couldn't participate for most of the semester. I remember one day of victory. I decided to try and make a three-point basket. I was playing with the eleventh grade boys, all of whom were much taller than me. I made the shot. The boys always said, "Wow" in unison. Jerold was so surprised that he was speechless. Then he said, "Damn. *Damn.*" I was in shock myself. Greta was really speechless. I was happy for the rest of the day.

U.S. History was also frustrating. I was always good at History, even more so than English. That's why it was hard for me to figure out what was wrong. The teacher I had in the fall, Mrs. Kettel, and I did not understand each other at all. At first I wasn't doing well in her class. I got a "D." I forgot why I got a "D" but then my mom and the teacher decided I'd receive oral instructions and tests. After that I got "As" in her course. Just when we got to know each other Mrs. Kettel decided to leave Arrowsmith because she had conflicts with the administration over her contract.

The teacher I had for U.S. History in the spring wasn't willing to let me do my tests orally. He was breaking the law. He wasn't the first or the last teacher who refused to give me my accommodations for my learning disability under federal law. We had quizzes every Friday. On Thursdays we had Study Skills instead so we didn't have class. I felt like only having the course Mondays through Wednesdays didn't leave enough time to study for the exams. The weekly schedule, for lack of a better word, "sucked." I didn't really pay attention nor did I care about the Study Skills sessions because I was worried about History.

I remember writing a letter to the principal saying that this schedule of having class from Monday through Wednesday, having Study Skills on Thursday and having a quiz on Friday was not working. They laughed instead of trying to help me. I remember how angry I was with the administration about this. I was very angry at their mocking response.

Since U.S. History was a lecture course, and the teacher wouldn't let me record my notes, I failed a lot of tests. It wasn't just me, though. Everyone failed his quizzes. That's what happens when someone is hired too fast. It was because of the administration's lack of judgment that I got a "C" in the class. I was mad. When the end-of-the-year evaluations came out, me and the other eleventh graders got him fired by giving him a poor evaluation. My GPA lowered from a 3.5 to a 3.0. I got "As" and "Bs" in all of my other courses, though. I was just happy that eleventh grade was over.

I began twelfth grade in the fall of 1994. During the fall, I was having a difficult time figuring out where to go for college. I decided to go to the California College of Arts and Crafts. I chose CCAC (now called

California College of the Arts) because at that time I was really into drawing. I thought that I could possibly get a career in the visual arts. I was accepted there and awarded two scholarships for my writing and my drawing.

From October 8–15, 1994, I traveled to Germany for the second time. On this trip we went to Bonn (the former West Germany's capital), Berlin and Frankfurt. In Bonn I read at the American high school on a military base. The students whom I read to were eighth through twelfth graders and they were American citizens, yet they had been born all over the world. The eighth graders who took me to lunch were born in places like Germany, Switzerland, Zimbabwe, South Africa, China and the United States. While visiting Bonn I got to visit the Beethoven House and the *Bonner Münster* (the main church). Both are located in the *Münsterplatz* (the main plaza).

In Berlin, I read at John F. Kennedy High School in the Charlottenburg neighborhood. I was the youngest person ever to read through the Arts America Program, a program sponsored by the U.S. State Department. Berlin is my favorite international city. I got to visit the Bode Museum on the Museum Island of Berlin at night during the 1994 trip. The museum was named after its first curator, Wilhelm von Bode, in 1956 and was designed by Ernst von Ihne. The night sky made the Spree River look black. The buildings and lights reflected on the water. The building had a dome on top. I love domes. The building was made of marble and the staircase was second best to me after the San Francisco City Hall rotunda staircase. The Bode Museum closed down in 1997 for renovation and then reopened in 2006. It is one of my favorite museums in the world.

In Berlin I stayed on the main avenue (*Kurfurstendamm*). We often took the subway (the U-Ban or the S-Ban) to the *Tiergarten* (Zoo) station. The America House was located near there. I also visited the Jewish ghetto in the former East Berlin. That neighborhood has been restored since my last visit.

During the school year I had problems with my Government/ Economics teacher. There was this girl in my class named Katherine who he harassed a lot. She made this joke and said something like, "If you screw me once, shame on you, if you screw me twice, shame on me, if you screw me three times..."

"You're in heaven," was his reply.

He also made sick jokes. He said that his left hand was his date on the airplane, and when we watched campaign commercials, he showed us footage of two rhinoceroses having sex. One of my friends who took the eighth-grade American History class said that he showed *Playboy* films. He got fired at the end of the year because of all of this and because during the senior trip, when he was supposed to chaperone, he bought alcohol for minors.

Once he gave us a packet that discussed, "Is inequality beneficial to society?" My father was mad. The next week we were chosen to debate it. Greta said that she wouldn't participate in the debate unless she was on the side that argued against inequality. Three of the people who argued on the other side were people of color. Two of them were immigrants from India and Iran. The third was an African-American named Jerold who once said that the NAACP was a "joke."

Suraj, who was born in India, was nasty to a lot of people. He didn't like black people, gay people and even immigrants. He said something nasty to one of my friends who happened to be gay. He told him, "Stop being so politically correct and go play with your multicultural pens." (Multicultural pens were a brand of pen made by Crayola at the time, which were supposed to be used for representing peoples' skin colors from very pale to very dark.) Kaveh and Jerold laughed. His nastiness wasn't personal to me. He disrespected Greta a lot of the time. Suraj was an obnoxious person. He either went off on people in a really nasty way or he laughed at people for no apparent reason. I don't know if these behaviors had to do with him being a teacher or if it was just part of his personality. He didn't have any respect towards others. I think he had self-hatred, so he didn't respect himself.

In the economics debate, Suraj said that students who attend public schools were "bad." He said that black, Latino, and Southeast Asian students who attend the public schools were biologically inferior to South Asians, Far East Asians and white students who attend the more affluent schools. Therefore, inequality was beneficial to society, in his mind. He also said that black and Chicano kids are prone to violence. Greta got angry and responded with a lot of facts. He was so surprised that he couldn't finish his argument.

There was also the Iranian kid, Kaveh, who thought he was better than other immigrants were. Kaveh told me that the town he lived in, a place called Alamo, was all white except for him. He supported Proposition 187, which had passed in the fall of 1994 in California, cutting off education and health care to children of "illegal aliens." Now that 9/11 has happened I hope that he changed his tune because the country he is from, Iran, is on Bush's "Axis of Evil" list.

In eleventh grade, I had liked the woman who taught British Literature. During this year, she taught American Literature. I like some Western literature like *Beowulf*, Chaucer and Louisa May Alcott, who wrote *Little Women*. I visited the house Alcott wrote about in *Little Women* located in Concord, Massachusetts. These writers influenced my poetry. But I had a problem with the teaching of literature written by whites exclusively. I was sick of reading the same thing year after year. But our teacher didn't want to try anything new. She told us that she "didn't want to be politically correct" and that she was "sorry if that offended anyone." She didn't sound sorry to me, and it did offend me. I couldn't say anything because I was shocked. I also felt sad that this person I looked up to betrayed me.

This teacher often became over-emotional. She came to class one day crying because two girls were teasing her. I don't remember what they said. She was prone to nervous breakdowns and would wind up in the ER. The administration let her go in the fall of 1998 after all of that.

I also had trouble in my Spanish class. My teacher was very difficult to work with. She was anti-disabled. She held the assumption, which a lot of immigrants and Americans have as well, that learning disabilities have to do with intelligence. I found many of her behaviors disturbing. I got "As" and "Bs" in her class, but she was angry with me because I struggled with past tense verbs. I ended up not taking her finals. She was rude towards people who had any form of learning disability. She addressed one my fellow classmates as "stupid." He had Dyslexia. Then, when he tried to defend himself, she got angry and told him not to talk back to her. I don't know how the whole thing ended. I also got ridiculed for not learning something as fast as she wanted me to. Doubting my abilities when I did well on a paper she asked me, "Did someone help you with this?" She shouted at one young man, *"No comprende!"* all of the time when he replied to her questions in English. He had severe learning disabilities that made speaking in Spanish difficult for him. At the end of each semester each teacher was asked to hand out awards for her classes. She always gave the same two people the awards. I gave her a poor evaluation. The other problem I had with Spanish class was a sugar low. We didn't eat lunch until 1:15 PM. I have a low blood sugar problem, meaning I get sick if I wait too long to eat. Normal lunch times are 11:45 AM or 12:00 PM. Arrowsmith was anti-disabled in a number of ways, even though they advertised themselves as being pro-individualized education methods. They broke a lot of ADA rules, like no wheelchair-accessible classrooms and anti-disabled teachers. Shouldn't teachers be screened to determine whether or not they have discrimination towards different groups of people, especially when social service agencies are recommending the school to parents as a good place for students needing special accommodations?

My Physics teacher was also a problem. He tried to make the class interesting, but since it was a straight lecture course it didn't capture my attention. He talked positively about Charles Murray's book *The Bell Curve*, which cast African-Americans as being intellectually inferior to whites. Jerold and me were the only two black people in the class. When he said this, we looked at each other in amazement. I don't know which schools right-wingers are talking about when they say that public education is overrun with liberals. That hasn't been my experiences, nor, I suspect, the experiences of most black and Latino students.

There was something I found confusing about my report cards. I usually would get "Bs" in my courses. An evaluation came with the grades and the notes were very positive. They never said there was anything I need to improve on or add to my work in order to receive an "A." From what the teachers wrote in their notes, I thought I should be getting straight "As." This is a mystery that will never be solved. Arrowsmith closed at the end of the 2005–2006 school year due to financial and administrative difficulties. Each year I was there, there was a different administration. Mom had taught at Arrowsmith Academy from 1990–2000. She said that Arrowsmith Academy did not treat the Drama course with the same seriousness as the academic courses. Because of that she decided to resign in 2000, right before her hip replacement. Her teaching there invited much publicity from the press. My father's play *Mother Hubbard*, directed by my mom, was performed there. This performance convinced Miguel Algarin to produce it off-Broadway in New York. This time Rome Neal directed it. During one off-Broadway performance Mary Wilson of the "Supremes" was in the audience. She asked for a role and received one.

On June 9, 1995 I graduated from high school and began the big transition to college.

CHAPTER SEVEN

California College Of Arts And Crafts

URING THE SUMMER OF 1995, I TOOK TWO CLASSES AT THE California College of Arts and Crafts, now called California College of the Arts. I took Drawing in the mornings from 9–12, and Painting from 1–4. The classes were okay. I don't really remember much about them, but they didn't show me how CCAC really was. I got "Cs" in both of the classes. I was glad that fall was on its way soon and I thought it was going to be better, but I was wrong. In the fall of 1995 I began to fall apart again. I had a hard time at CCAC. I liked my English and Basic Drawing classes, because the teachers, Richard Oyama and Eleanor Dickinson, were excellent, but I didn't like my 2-D and 3-D classes.

I had 3-D on Fridays from 8–2. The teacher made one comment saying, "You should learn to draw some more." His personality was hard for me to figure out. I'm not sure if he said that out of frustration or if it was just a joke since a few months before the school had given me a scholarship award for my creativity. We had 8:00 AM "homeroom" sessions, where we would discuss our experiences in our class. I mentioned the comment "You should learn to draw some more." I don't remember the reaction it received from our mentor, however a young man and a young woman said they were bothered by the comment. I don't really remember anything about the 3-D course besides that. I remember a couple of my projects. We used the shop a lot. I used an electric drill, a circular saw and a table saw. Usually I don't like the sounds these machines make, but when I am the one making these sounds they don't bother me.

At least my 3-D teacher acknowledged my learning disability. I wrote my 2-D teacher a letter describing my learning disability. He never acknowledged it. He had us cast a bronze piece, which is the subject of 3-D class. I asked my friends who were taking 2-D classes with another teacher if they were doing bronze pieces and working with wood. None were.

The professor was frustrated with me because I had trouble with multiple step directions. He kept explaining the directions to me in the same way. When I still didn't get it, he said, "Why don't you understand this? It's so easy." The freshman class at CCAC was people who were ages thirty to forty-five, mostly. There were only three other eighteen-year-olds beside me. The adults were experienced at how to design the projects that were assigned, but I had never done anything like this before. I don't know how I did it, but I finally completed the project. I still have it. I don't remember anything else about that course.

During mid-term week in the middle of October he called me a "burden to him and the rest of the class." (The $2,000 I paid for his class was a burden on me.) That's when I decided to drop the class. I also dropped 3-D. The only positive thing that came out of that class was learning how to use tools.

I could tell that there was something wrong around late September because none of my teachers knew the nature of my learning disability. When I enrolled in classes that spring, my counselor told me that she would write a letter and put it in my teachers' boxes. I didn't know my mentor would be Opal Palmer Adisa, a Jamaican author and a friend of my friends Kathryn Takara and Karla Brundage, who has served as Chair of Ethnic Studies and the Cultural Diversity Program at CCAC. I didn't meet with her until late October or early November since I had dropped 2-D and 3-D. It was already too late then.

In mid-October of 1995 my mother, my father, and I had a discussion with Liz, the Dean of Students and Bill, the Head of the counseling program, I told them my experience with the teachers. Bill brought up an incident that happened when I went to summer school there, and asked me if I weren't overreacting a little bit. I had become familiar with this pattern. Like the police and their "blue wall of silence," teachers are reluctant to critique their colleagues. Unfortunately, I don't remember all of the details of the incident. He also told me that my 3-D teacher was disappointed that I left his class, but he said that he understood. My 2-D teacher's reaction was: "Well, I hope that you have a big success in life."

I was also disturbed by the mean-spirited competition between the students. My friend, who thought that O.J. Simpson was innocent of murdering his wife Nicole, and her date, Ron Goldman, was called a "bitch." The O.J. criminal trial was winding to a close in September of 1995. She was Jewish and black as well. The school was mostly made up of upper class white students. My friend also said that one student said that there were no smart black people and that they couldn't speak "correct" English. This student also said that black people couldn't "make art." My dad was furious about these attitudes. He went up to CCAC and lectured the whole assembly about racism and O.J., based on Richard Wright's character Bigger Thomas. During the question and answer period nobody challenged him.

I liked my Basic Drawing teacher, Eleanor Dickinson. She liked my kind of drawings. I looked forward to her class. She liked the fact that I drew differently than the other students. She learned a lot from me and I learned a lot from her. This was the only class where I had self-confidence and where I had a real interaction with my classmates. I had fun drawing the assignments. I got to work with Conte crayons, charcoal, colored pencils, chalk and markers. Before this, most of my drawings were made with felt tip markers and colored pencils. There were no uncomfortable incidents in this course.

In the middle of the semester Professor Dickinson invited us to her home in San Francisco for a party. Her children and grandchildren were there. It was a really nice party. I don't remember what I ate, who all was there or most of what my conversations were about, but I remember one conversation with her eight-year-old granddaughter about my cat "Happy" eating dust off of the floor. I also remember Professor Dickinson's art studio in the basement, which was directly under the living room. There were a lot sculptures. I noticed that she liked to use a lot of colors and that her art was considered "abstract." I really liked her animal sculptures, especially the one of birds.

I also liked my Basic English course taught by writer and professor Richard Oyama. My dad and Professor Oyama had known each other for a long time. They had met in New York. The class reader was similar to the ones that I used later on at Cal. I don't remember what we read. He had us write essays, which was a weak form for me. One day we had ran into Professor Oyama at Safeway on Broadway and 51st. He said that I "didn't know how to write an essay." Dad was upset about that comment but when I entered Laney I realized that this was true and so did Dad. As I continued at Laney, after CCAC, my essay writing strengthened.

I dropped out of CCAC in December of 1995. Before that my parents met with the President of CCAC, who called for an investigation of my experience there. As a result, he reprimanded the teachers with whom I had difficulty and instituted reforms so that students with learning disabilities wouldn't have to suffer. He said I could create my own curriculum, but I decided not to return. Ever since my experience there, more minority-race students have enrolled at CCAC, and I may have changed the lives of the people with learning disabilities who attend CCAC for the better.

CHAPTER EIGHT

Laney College

APPLIED TO LANEY COLLEGE IN DECEMBER OF 1995. I CHOSE Laney, a community college in Oakland because I wanted to avoid taking the SATs. I also picked Laney because the Disabled Students Programs and Services were said to be very good there. I entered Laney College still bitter and angry from my experience at CCAC. I was worried that I might have trouble with some of the professors there also. It went much smoother than I thought. I made a lot of friends and I did well in a majority of my classes except for English 1B.

In English 1B my professor was Professor Rezendez. Professor Rezendez had known me since I was a little kid because her daughter, Sierra, was in my 1/2 class at Park School. I didn't remember her but I did remember Sierra who was a freshman at UCLA that year. Professor Rezendez, a feminist, also knew my father.

Professor Rezendez assigned us essays asking us what our opinions were on certain topics. I don't remember what the first essay I wrote was about, but I had followed the instructions and done at least five revisions on the essay. At first, I was just quoting people instead of using my own words and creativity. The problem was I didn't know how to analyze essays. Instead, I summarized the essays because that was what I was taught to do at a very young age.

It didn't make sense to me why I got a "C," even when I followed her instructions or when I did the revisions she asked me to do. A couple of years later it began to make sense. In my Intro to Sociology course in the spring of 1998 I chose one of the three questions for our midterm, which I forgot, and decided to write an essay about how the English professors graded papers on whether or not their students agreed with their point of view. It brought back memories of middle school when I was graded on how I interpreted the stories and poems.

Some professors tended to reward good grades to the students who agreed with them, even if those same students didn't show up to class or didn't do the work. These were mostly white students. These professors tended to give lower grades to the people who didn't agree with them, even when we showed up to class and did the work. I received a "C" in that course. Look at it this way, I had published an essay in my dad's anthology, "*MultiAmerica,*" and had been praised by his editor, Don Fehr, and famous writers such as Rudolfo Anaya, Adrienne Kennedy, Simon Ortiz, Al Young and John A. Williams, but I got "Cs" in English. Go figure.

During the summer Dad was invited to Japan for a fifteen-day tour on behalf of his book *Japanese by Spring.* Therefore, I got to visit Japan for my second time. We were in Japan from June 14–June 30, 1996. We went to Tokyo, Kyoto, Kobe, Hiroshima, Fukuoka, Nagoya and Sapporo. We spent most of the trip in Kyoto. I enjoyed Kyoto the best because it had older architecture. I visited the temples Kinkaku-ji (or Golden Pavilion), Ginkaku-ji (or Silver Pavilion), Ryoanji (with its famous Zen rock garden) and Sanjusangendo Hall with the 1,001 golden images. We visited the Emperor's Palace where a group of high school-aged-children interviewed me for their English class. While in Kyoto Mom and I traveled to Osaka by express train to visit Suzushi Hanayagi. We visited the house I stayed in when Mom took me to Japan as a baby.

In Hiroshima we visited the Peace Park and Museum, where we went on a tour with a survivor of the Hiroshima bombings. That was the first time I really felt ashamed of being an American. We also visited Miyagima Island where we took a little boat to visit the aquarium.

At the University of Sapporo on the island of Hokaido, I got to read my poetry. We also got to visit Otaru while we were in Sapporo. On the way up we could see Russia across the Sea of Japan. It was a beautiful city that reminded me of San Francisco. In Sapporo we had dinner a couple of times with American diplomats. They said some pretty offensive things like, "Oh, the Japanese are such clean people. They never sweat." One man married a Japanese woman and just had a baby. The baby was born with brown eyes, he stated, and now they were a blue-gray. He was happy about it. "What's wrong with brown eyes?" I asked. "Do you think people who have brown eyes are ugly?" He didn't answer the question. Instead, he said, "My wife is very happy about that as well." I said, "Your wife has some self-hatred." He didn't answer. The same gentleman drove us in his SUV to Otaru the next day. He played some music from a CD. I forget who the name of the artist. He sounded like he was singing the chant of some Native American tribes. "Is this artist Native American?" Dad asked the gentleman. "No," he replied. "I can see a lot of people becoming offended over this song," said Dad. That was the end of that conversation.

I wrote a poem about my Japanese travels.

NIHON NO RYOKO
(JAPANESE TRAVEL)

You can't always take the airline
you want to take like American or TWA
Sometimes you have to take whatever's cheaper
like United or Northwest

You can't always
sit by the window
on the airplane
Sometimes you have to sit
by the aisle or in the middle

You can't always get
American food
like hamburgers, pizza
eggs and ham
Sometimes you can
only eat Japanese food like
sushi, teriyaki, sunomono and chawanmushi

You can't stay in one place
all of the time
Sometimes you have to Shinkansen to or from
a new city daily
like Osaka or Tokyo

You can't always find clunky-heeled loafer
Japanese school girl shoes

in your size in Kobe or Kyoto
Sometimes you have to go to Nagoya
to find them

You can't always rely on following the schedule
like when I was told
we would go exploring in the morning
or eat at a certain restaurant
sometimes you have to accept
last minute change
like when our guide decided to choose
a restaurant where we sat on tatami mats
instead of a Chinese restaurant
where we could sit on chairs like at home

You can't get a hotel room
with a big space like the Rihga Royal in Hiroshima
you sometimes have to stay in a tiny
hole-in-the-wall
like the Personal Hotel
in Fukuoka, where the price is good

You won't find the U.S. everywhere,
but you will find courteous people everywhere
safe streets and subways at night full of people having fun
the walking signal on traffic lights
playing "Coming Through the Rye"
and 1001 golden images at Sanjusangendo
moats surrounding the walls of Nijo Castle
red, yellow and white triangles
on selected high rise glass skyscrapers
the mixture of gray rock, raked granite
and luscious green gardens
at the Silver Pavilion
the stork, with his beak striped in pastels
like a Richard Diebenkorn painting
as he stares from a rock at the Miyajima Aquarium
and a herd of deer following you asking to be fed
on the beach at the Itsukushima Shrine

The fall of 1996 was a hard semester. I took Critical Thinking that
semester. My professor gave me a "C" on one of my essays written from
the point of view of a bell pepper. My dad thought it was brilliant. In

the summer of 2002, at the Atlantic Center for the Arts in New Smyrna Beach, Florida, I wrote a poem about a bell pepper. It was published in my fourth poetry collection, *City Beautiful,* which was published in 2006. My dad was so upset that he sent the professor something called the "Ishmael Reed" letter. These letters are so insulting to the person or institution that sometimes he doesn't mail them out. My mother often tells him to take a deep breath before sending out these letters, but very often, these letters get results. Dad is usually cool, but this time he wasn't. He told the professor that there should be a restraining order preventing a teacher like him from coming within a mile of a creative person. The professor was so surprised that this was the first time I saw him speechless. I was given a "C" or "C-" on my papers, even though I did the revisions that he told me to do. Some of the students would never show up to class or group meetings and they got "As" and "Bs." In fact, one young woman did the group project by herself because all of her group mates had dropped out of class.

November of 1996 was a trying month. We were assigned a group project in my Critical Thinking class. I liked Gennelle and Niessa but I didn't get along with Lena, Matt and Christina. They were silly, which comes with becoming nineteen and twenty years old. Christina cussed me out in front of the class because I didn't call her up to tell her that there was a meeting. I just remember my partner, Lena, saying, "You didn't call her up and that's your job." They waited until 7AM on the morning before our oral presentation to get serious. I stayed at school that day between 7 AM in the morning and 4 PM in the afternoon. That was the day of my Biology lab. I was really tired. They were mad at me because I didn't come to the last meeting at ten that night. I was coming down with a cold and stomach virus and I needed the energy for the presentation. Thanksgiving was two days later. Christina called me up at seven telling me that I had to come. I told her I was the only one who hadn't missed a meeting and that I was tired from such a long day. That month I complained all the time about the group project. My friend Michael told me to not get stressed out. Easier said than done.

The oral presentation went well. After the presentation we were required to write a personal essay about our experiences with the group project. I had already started it, but during the Thanksgiving weekend I got to vent my anger towards my former group mates. I got another "C" on the essay. I felt that things like attendance, work and studying didn't matter to teachers any more.

The spring semester of 1997 was much better. I enjoyed all of my classes.

One started out poorly, though. The teacher was hired at the last minute and soon began sexually harassing some of the girls in the class. I witnessed one girl being touched on the breast after class. Another girl had this happen in his office as well. He asked one girl to spread her legs. He told her that if she did she would get an automatic "A." He asked another girl to kiss him on the cheek. After our first exam I asked him if we had any homework. He was leaning toward me uncomfortably close. He rubbed his hands up and down another student's arm and used her leg to help him stand up. Four other people besides me went up to the Dean and complained. Immediate action followed.

I called up a friend and told him that I was having trouble with this professor. My friend's name was Michael and he was forty eight-year-old black Vietnam veteran. I had met him through the Disabled Students' Program. I don't know what the nature of his disability was. He had seven children (three boys and four girls) ranging in age from seven to thirty. He also had two granddaughters ages seven and three months. At first he was out of it and didn't pay attention to what I had to say. After thinking it over for a few minutes, he called back and said, "That dude is sick. He's got to go." So he and I went to the Dean.

The Dean of the Instructors came and looked at the class. He wasn't making any physical contact. The next class was cancelled. All of the students who didn't know what was going on were upset with those of us who complained. They only wanted their Associate's Degree and felt that we had taken our sexual harassment complaint too far. The teacher was put on leave with pay.

I didn't have any more problems with my professors or my classmates. That was the semester when I did the best work. The problem I had during the spring was with the people in the Learning Skills Program.

With learning and physical disabilities come emotional problems. I know because I have a lot of emotional problems myself, including anger, jealousy and insecurity.

The Disabled Program had a club called the United Students with Abilities. Our club's mission was to learn to socialize with people. It didn't work because I had trouble getting along with some of the members. We fought most of the semester about where we were going on the school trip. A couple of people were upset that we didn't go to the Manteca waterslides like they wanted.

We finally decided on the Santa Cruz Beach Boardwalk. We raised money for this trip by attending High School Day, the day students from high schools visited the campus. There was always a big crowd. We sold pizza, candy, chocolate chip cookies, and soda to teenagers. They went for our table more than the other clubs' tables. Michael had made the reservations to Santa Cruz for 9 to 5. A couple of people got angry with him, telling him that it would take three hours to get there and that we would only have three hours to go on rides. He was intending to stay longer. At the next club meeting Michael apologized. Evidently, two other members of the club were unhappy because of the reservations. One of them decided to go to Michael's Algebra class to pick a fight with him. Michael was very upset, so much so that he took it out on his wife and kids. He said that he shouted at them so loud that he had to close the windows and door so the neighbors wouldn't hear them. I think that Michael had a right to be angry.

One of the other club members, who was a friend of the club member who cussed Michael out, decided to take it out on me for what Michael did to him. I think that she was afraid to take her anger out on Michael because he was really tall and older, and therefore, she didn't want to mess with him. She spread rumors about me to her friends, telling them that I did Michael's paper for him, which almost led to a physical confrontation between her and me. It definitely did a lot of damage to our relationship. All I did was lend him some of my anatomy books. He had gotten an "A" on his paper. When he showed her the paper she said, "Well!" and left the room in a huff.

The trip day went from 9AM to 9PM including traveling time. Michael brought four of his kids and one of his kid's friends on the trip. Nicky and Jesse, these two club members who were sometimey when it came to any type of relationship, were upset because they didn't want anyone younger than twelve on the bus. Their reason was that they had to "watch what they say," or "they would run around the bus and make noise," and many other stupid reasons. Michael brought his seven-year-old daughter, April, his ten-year-old daughter, Anice, his eleven-year-old son, Joe, along with his friend Desmond and his twelve-year-old daughter, Winona. One of the older girls got their feelings hurt and asked, "Why aren't the adults talking to us?" The kids behaved very well on the trip. I hung out with them. It was a great day. I ended the school year still quite angry at Nicky. Our relationship had mended a little bit, but there was anger, hurt and distrust, at least on my part. I got two "As" and a "B" though, the best I had done at Laney so far.

In the fall of 1997, my International Relations professor was the kind of professor who didn't like his students to challenge his beliefs and didn't want his students to voice their opinions. I guess that's what he meant when he intended his class to be "politically incorrect." He showed us films like *Braveheart* with Mel Gibson about the thirteenth-century Scots trying to overthrow English rule, and *Evita* with Madonna about Evita Duarte, the wife of Argentinean president Juan Peron. He talked about prostitution a lot. In fact he was obsessed with it. I wanted to learn more about African, Asian and South American history. He used a quote from Hitler's *Mein Kampf* that said,

"We must clearly recognize the fact that the recovery of the lost territories is not won through solemn appeals to the Lord or through pious hopes in a League of Nations, but only by force of arms." (Hitler, Adolf. *Mein Kampf*. Wilmington, MA: Mariner Books, 1998.)

He said that in this case Hitler was right. This young black woman and I looked at each other and said, "Did he just say Hitler was right?" Laney College had a high minority enrollment. In fact the average student at

Laney was a thirty-year old African-American female. But that didn't mean the school was immune from the kinds of bigotry that teachers have toward people of color.

This professor was quite arrogant. We spent most of the semester getting ready for our final paper. I don't remember anything about the paper. It counted as a high percentage of our overall grade. We discussed our ideas for our paper one night. I don't remember what he said or I said, but I remember feeling frustrated by his arrogance. He told everybody in the course that if we didn't add that one key factor in our paper, which I think was a clear and concise thesis paragraph, "I'm going to give out an 'F.' People can call to complain and cry and I'll just listen." He was full of attitude. Amazingly, I got a "B" out of the class.

Things could have been worse for me, though. My friend Maria, who was a mixture of Cherokee Indian and Puerto Rican, complained that there was a history teacher at Laney College who used to belong to a KKK organization down in Louisiana. The teacher hated Indians, blacks and Asians. First of all I wanted to know who hired him, and second of all, why was he teaching at Laney? This teacher said that what white people did to the black people during slavery times was benign and that what they did to the Native Americans was all right because white people rule the world and own the land.

Most of the time we talked about race in my English and Sociology classes that I took in the spring of 1998. Professor Wilson taught my English 1A course. I forgot what the name of the young woman who taught my sociology course. She was half Mexican and half Filipina. That's all I remember. The Rodney King incident, during which members of the Los Angeles Police Department were caught on videotape beating Rodney King, came up in my Sociology class. A young white man said that Rodney King "got what he deserved" and "when you're on PCP and crack you don't feel anything." He also argued that Rodney King decked a police officer, which was inaccurate. When a young black woman and young black man started arguing with him, the professor became angry.

She said, "May I please have the floor?" She told them to "think like sociologists and ask questions instead of arguing."

The following Monday our teacher showed us a film about how sociologists obtain facts. The film's argument was that people who live in the "slums" have a higher chance of becoming criminals than people in middle- and upper-class neighborhoods. They showed a young black man being arrested by two white officers. The next scene was about welfare and they showed black and Latino mothers with their babies. Then to add insult to injury they showed a Filipino couple in suburban New York with their two children living the American dream. The truth is that Filipinos are among the poorest Asian-Americans and that 80 per cent of people on welfare are white.

The next Wednesday we were put into our Sociology groups. Unfortunately, I was assigned to work with the kid who said that nasty comment about Rodney King and two other males who believed that men are superior to women. Anyway, we discussed what we wanted to do but none of us could agree with each other. The kid who said that racist comment about Rodney King said that economic inequality is beneficial to society. That sounded like those three boys in high school. I called him a Nazi. That's what first got him angry. The teacher, seeing that most of the groups were having a hard time agreeing with something, assigned us our arguments. My group was told to argue that women are not inferior to men. A couple of the boys got upset and said that men are superior to women and said that women should have to obey men. I called them Promise Keepers. This made the students even angrier and I didn't really care either. Later we discussed an exercise that we had to do in the book. The kid got even angrier and had a tantrum. He felt that no one wanted to listen to him. He backed his chair up and almost ran over another student. You just have to laugh at people like that.

In English class a young black woman said, "The reason why this country is too overpopulated is because all Asians and Latinos have too many children." I said, "Well, you have to understand what religious background they came from." Instead of getting angry, she said, "Well, that's true." When we read an essay in class one Asian woman made a good point. She said that the reason why they cut off emergency medical service as well as education and bilingual education to immigrants in California is because some white people still want to be the majority and are afraid of being the "minority." The white people in the class started squirming uncomfortably in their seats.

As I said before, I not only get racism from black people and white people, but from Asians and Latinos as well. There was a racist Korean woman in my English class. She had attitude problems with me for reasons that I couldn't understand. She was pretty right wing. She said that she had a high paying job. She said that Affirmative Action had helped her get her job, but she voted against Affirmative Action when it was on the California ballot. I asked her, "Well why did you vote against it if it helped you?" Her answer was, "Well, it wouldn't help African-Americans or Latinos because they are lazy, they do drugs, they listen to that rap shit, they drink, and they don't want to do anything constructive. Personally, I don't like African-Americans. Asian people and white people always want to do something for themselves." I answered, "Well I'm half black, and I have traveled all over the world reading my poetry, and I go to school. There are a lot of intelligent black and Latino people. Your friend Flore is black. Why don't you hate her?"

"Because she is from Africa, she is not an African-American."

"So basically you are saying that you want to cut off Affirmative Action because you got yours and therefore you are in fear that an African-American or a Latino might rise to your level and that you want them to stay at the level they are?" She said, "Well...yes." I said, "You're a mother... right?" She nodded. I said, "Are you going to tell that to your children?" All of my friends started laughing at her and she looked really bad.

I loved my Sociology class and I maintained an "A" average in the class. The English class was where I felt the most uncomfortable. I decided that if I got into U.C. Berkeley that I wasn't going to take English courses. My English professor felt that she had to give me low grades because I didn't agree with her point of view. She was arrogant and silly. One day she told me that she'd "always have the last word," meaning that she would be grading our papers. She thought she was being funny. One Thursday she told the class that she had to dock people if they didn't understand the writer's point of view even though they wrote a good essay. I explained to her, on behalf of most of the class, that the writer's point of view was not clear. I don't remember the author or the essay. She rudely interrupted me with a tone of voice saying that if I had read the story four or five times I would have understood the writer's point of view. I told her that I did read it four or five times and that the writing was still unclear.

I had a hard time getting along with some people in this class because of their outright bigotry. There was one girl, who was one of my best friends in the class, but her political views were to the right. We were talking about Proposition 227, a law put on the ballot in California banning bilingual education in the schools. Note that three quarters of the class were immigrants. They were giving her dirty looks. She said that she didn't think the law was a threat to the survival of other languages or that it would handicap immigrant children. I disagreed. As a person of semitic, black, Asian, white and Native American ancestry that law offended me. My semitic (Jewish) ancestors were prevented from speaking Hebrew and Yiddish, the languages of my African ancestors were stamped out, my Asian ancestors were prohibited from coming to California for many years and my Cherokee ancestors were removed forcibly from the eastern U.S. and also had to assimilate into white culture. Not only did they have to give up their language, customs and religion, but also they were exploited, tortured and beaten if they practiced their religion, spoke their language and dressed in their traditional clothes.

Outside of school I worked for Dad five hours a week. I clipped out articles and categorized them. I continue to help with his research when he's working on a project. One of my jobs was to also visit the elderly people on the block. I took my interest in community affairs seriously. I was elected secretary of the Market Street Corridor. We met once a month at the site of the old Merritt College on Martin Luther King, Jr. Way. Guest speakers came to talk to us and we also discussed neighborhood problems with the Oakland Police and elected officials. I also wrote. I decided to socialize less at Laney and focus more on my studies since I wanted to boost my grade point average and obtain my Associate's

Degree. I had earned nearly all of my General Education requirements for my major, which was going to be Liberal Arts if I had decided to remain at Laney instead of transferring to U.C. Berkeley.

I was very optimistic in the fall of 1997 when my counselor told me that I should acquire my AA degree even though I was transferring to a four-year institution. I was only one requirement short and nine units short, which I could make up during the summer. That's what she said.

On Friday, April 3, 1998, however, she told me that she had made a mistake and that I was twenty units short. She said that I should wait to hear from Berkeley and if I wasn't accepted I should possibly enroll for the fall 1998 semester at Laney. When I got home, Dad called up my counselor at Berkeley, Naima Jahi. She was upset and told Dad that I was "being targeted" by my counselor at Laney. On Tuesday, April 7, 1998, I went with Dad to see the Dean of Student Services to discuss the matter. I was very confused. The Dean examined my transcript on his computer and told me that all of my courses at Laney, including the courses I was currently taking, added up to fifty-eight-and-a-half out of sixty units. He told me that he would see if I could get credits from my English class at CCAC. He also checked to see if I had completed my General Ed course requirements like the life and physical sciences, the humanities and art requirements and other courses. I had completed all of the GE courses except for the computer class.

On Friday, April 10, the Dean of Student Services told me that I was lacking ten-and-a-half units instead of the twenty that my counselor had come up with. He had counted the remedial courses that weren't counted toward the AA degree. He told me that I could take Computer Literacy in the summer, which would add one more unit.

I was told that in order to go to U.C. Berkeley I needed four transferable credits from at least two of the following areas:

1) The Arts and Humanities (my Art History and Values and Ethics classes)

2) The Social Behavioral Sciences (my intro to African-American Studies class and my Psychology class)

3) The Physical and Biological Sciences (my Intro to Astronomy and
Intro to Biology classes)

He also told me that I had to meet these requirements with a "C" or better and that in the fall of 1998, I could take nine and a half more units at Laney. That meant I had to wait until the fall of 1999 to go to Cal because they didn't accept students in the spring. I would have to apply again.

I enrolled in Human Sexuality, the Psychology of Childhood, the U.S. Since 1945, and Body Conditioning. That all added up to ten and a half units. I decided not to walk the stage with the AA candidates because at the time I didn't know whether or not I was going to be accepted to Berkeley. Then, the letter came from Cal. I was accepted, so I decided to transfer to Cal instead of getting my AA. I was ready to move on. I finished Laney on May 21, 1998. I got an "A" in Sociology and a "B" in English. I dropped all of the other classes I was planning to take at Laney. I was going to enter Berkeley as a sophomore/junior.

I didn't go on the school trip to Great America Amusement Park. I didn't attend the United Students with Abilities Club party as well. My counselor stopped speaking to me after the April incident. She seemed to resent the fact that I got into Cal. When I spoke to her, she ignored me. A person in the Dean's office said that the counselor had a "communication problem." I wonder how many blacks, Latinos, and Native Americans have been misled in their career goals as a result of bad counseling.

I returned my Statement of Legal Residence and my Statement of Intention to Register for Berkeley in late April or early May along with my housing application. I was assigned the Clark Kerr Residence Hall, Building Twelve. In June, I attended the Alumni reception. In July I attended Cal Student Orientation Day. After that I traveled to New Mexico for a second time visiting Albuquerque, Santa Fe, Los Alamos, Pecos National Historical Park, Bandelier National Monument, Espanola and the Puye Ruins.

CHAPTER NINE

U.C. Berkeley

WASN'T TOO THRILLED TO MOVE INTO THE DORMITORY ON AUGUST 16, 1998, I must say, because transferring to a new school was about as much change as I could take. My parents thought it would be a good idea for me to stay in the dorms, so I could learn how to live on my own. I would have liked to stay at home and commute on AC Transit to school. At Cal we had a class pass, so taking the bus was free. The F bus would pick me up right down the street from my home on 53rd Street and drop me off at Bancroft below Telegraph near the main entrance. I'm sure that I would have eaten better, slept better, stayed healthier and my GPA would have been much higher if I was able to study at home without dealing with the noise of the freshmen talking loudly and running in the hall. In a perfect world, I would have helped my parents turn the entire upstairs into an apartment, get a job, pay rent, share the laundry room with them, pay for my groceries, make my own meals and study in my room. This is not a perfect world.

I didn't socialize with anybody at the dorm, nor did I attend the Sunday night dorm meetings with the residence hall assistant. I was bored, lonely and upset. I didn't eat or sleep because of the noise. I ate junk food and I couldn't study. The lack of sleep and the junk food made me cranky all of the time. Luckily, I was close enough to home to go home during the weekends, on school holidays and during the winter, spring and summer vacations. I especially didn't like the food served at the dining commons that looked like it had been sitting there for days and wasn't properly cooked. I was worried about catching meningitis or mononucleosis. I didn't like having to share a foul co-ed bathroom with twenty other people. Clark Kerr is rated the best dorm on campus, but I didn't like it at all. I could tell that my dorm mates thought I was weird for not socializing with them. I didn't care. The age difference didn't help. I was twenty-one and a half and most of them were eighteen.

On January 12, 1999, I moved into a private residence three blocks north of Clark Kerr. The new place was called Barrows House. Halfway though the fall semester, a friend of my family friends Hillel and Eva, whose name was Alex, told me about it and said he would try and get me in for the spring. It wasn't a dormitory *per se*, it was in between a dormitory and a co-op. I had my own room and there was less walking. The building was much smaller than the one at Clark Kerr and I didn't have to share the bathroom with that many people. Unlike a regular apartment all the utilities were paid for. The rent was around $425 a month, while Clark Kerr was $858 a month. The Clark Kerr administration said I still had to pay the $858 a month until someone moved into the room I had abandoned. Someone did immediately. At Barrows House, I had to renew my lease each semester. I stayed there the remaining two and a half school years at Cal. Just like with Clark Kerr, I went home on weekends, school holidays and during the winter, spring and summer vacations, although I spent much of my summer vacation studying in England during the year 2000. I always had the same room at the Barrow's House, room #109.

After a week of orientation, I started classes on August 24, 1998, a Monday. I only liked one of my classes. That class was African-American Essays taught by the late Professor Barbara Christian, author of *Black Women Novelists*, winner of an American Book Award, and co-editor of the *Norton Anthology of African-American Literature*. She was the ex-wife of poet David Henderson, Jimi Hendrix's biographer. My parents both knew Professor Christian and David from their New York days. Professor Christian was from St. Thomas in the U.S. Virgin Islands. We read books by W.E.B. Du Bois, Audre Lorde, James Baldwin and Alice Walker. The teacher was able to answer our questions. A well-known scholar, Professor Christian knew her stuff and respected our opinions. For all of her celebrity she was very modest.

The late Professor Christian behaved much differently from the other professors I had in the African-American Studies department. I didn't feel uncomfortable around Professor Christian so I participated much more in her class than most of the other classes I took at Cal. Professor Christian treated me very well. She took the time to help me write a strong research paper on Anna Julia Cooper's book, *A Voice from the South*, written in 1882. Ms. Cooper lived until she was 105 years old. After looking at Professor Christian's corrections, I realized that I hadn't been taught the proper way to write a paper at Laney. She never put me down or raised her voice at me. I also liked her young GSI (or Graduate Student Instructor), a beautiful tall, thin African-American woman. She was one of the very few dark-skinned African-Americans I have encountered who didn't give me any problems for being light skinned. I noticed that both the GSI and Professor Christian were secure women, who are few and far between in this world. Professor Christian died in June of 2000 of lung cancer while I was in England. During the time I took her course she was coughing a lot. The doctors dismissed it as Bronchitis and gave her antibiotics. She was still coughing after the three week Bronchitis cough period. I told her to get another opinion and demanded that she get tests. Sure enough she did and was diagnosed with lung cancer. She smoked a lot. Dad said at her memorial that it was due to the pressures she was under as Chairperson of the African-American Studies Department, which was under-funded and beset with rivalries between Caribbean-Americans and traditional African-Americans.

The other two professors I had in that department were hostile to me. One was the late Professor VeVe Amasasa Clark who taught Caribbean Literature. She was upset because I used a tape recorder in her course and because of this she humiliated me before her class. I tried to explain to her that I needed the tape recorder in order to effectively absorb information. She didn't listen to what I had to say, or what the very few black men in class had to say, but she would acknowledge the black and white women. It amazes me how members of some oppressed groups refuse to recognize the problems of others.

Professor Clark wasn't clear when she gave us assignments. She was often unprepared and missed a lot of classes. Our first paper assignment was to analyze some essays in the reader. She told us we could choose any one of the essays in the reader to analyze. I forget what the essay was about, or what book I chose to write about, but she said to me, "That wasn't what I assigned. We need to talk." She then turned to a young white woman and started discussing a book by Edwidge Danticat, a famous young writer from Port-au-Prince, Haiti. I forgot what she said, or what the conversation was about but the young white woman started crying. Professor Clark approached her and hugged her saying, "Come here, baby. It's okay." In my opinion this was very inappropriate. I was already angry that she rejected my paper, but I was really disgusted at the scene between her and the young white woman. They were carrying on like she was Hattie MacDaniels, Scarlet O'Hara's maid in *Gone With the Wind*. The rest of the class was silent because they didn't know what to make of this odd scene, but I gave them both disgusted looks, and as many people who know me tell me, I wear my emotions on my face. I dropped her class that day and decided to change my major from African-American Studies to American Studies.

The late Professor Clark was a feminist, but apparently her feminism didn't have room for disabled and biracial women. She died on December 1, 2007, right before she turned sixty-three. I'm not sure how she died. She had diabetes and from what I heard she didn't take care of herself. She was a troubled individual. I felt sorry for her, even though our relationship was less than amicable. In her obituary dated December 14, 2007 (her birthday), that was printed in *The San Francisco Chronicle*, Professor Ula Taylor described Professor Clark as, "a personal cheerleader for many of the students, a kind, caring and generous member of our faculty. She was a woman of integrity with an encouraging spirit." That was not my impression of her, but everyone has different experiences.

The other class that I had problems with was my History of Africa class. The professor was boring. She was also hostile, but in a different way than Professor Clark. This professor was passive-aggressive and nervous. Her GSI was not that great either. The smell of incompetence and tension filled the room. The professor was from Kenya and her GSI was from India. I basically had no interest in her class. I only took the course because the courses I wanted were full, and there weren't many choices in the catalog under my major. I was stuck with this one. New students have to wait longer than continuing students to enroll in courses at Cal.

My grades showed my lack of interest in the course. I took the midterm and I failed. I took a make-up midterm in November, and again I failed. Luckily I had the opportunity to do a paper, so if I got an "A" on the paper it pulled my grade up to a "C." Having written and published since I was very young, I was more persuasive in expressing myself by narrative than by answering quiz questions.

I also had a chance to do well on the final. The reader had given me a "C" on the paper and a "D" on the final. I was beyond mad because I worked very hard on the paper and on studying for the final. The GSI came from an educational system that stressed an ancient English writing style. His questions on the paper were of the nitpicking variety. For example, when I wrote that one of the reasons Europe exploited Africa was for oil, he asked what type of oil. The reader said he gave me a "D" on the final because I didn't fill enough paper in the blue testing book. The instructions said that I would be graded on the content of the final, not on merely the length of my responses.

The students disrupted the class a lot because the professor's palpable fear gave them power over her. She lectured us with her eyes closed, although she opened her eyes one day, the Tuesday before Thanksgiving, and said, "You two, no conversation!" She was looking at two young women directly. The class was puzzled at how she knew who was having the conversation. Her lectures were painful to listen to. Her nervousness made me nervous. I always sat by the window, which was to my left, and watched the hundreds of people walk by Dwinelle Hall or I watched my fellow classmates.

In the spring of 1999, I complained about the grade I received on the paper I wrote. I asked for a meeting with the professor. I had received a "D." My father, a professor at Cal, accompanied me. She spoke to him alone at first, and then she met with both of us. She said that she'd read the paper and agreed that the grade was unfair and told us that she would change it. Dad told her that maybe East Indians shouldn't be grading my papers. "Do not go there, Professor," she replied. She said that it was a stereotype that some East Indians have racist attitude towards African Americans. "Well sometimes stereotypes hold true," Dad said with laughter. She also said that she'd offered me considerable help over the semester.

When I picked up my transcript a month later I found out that the grade hadn't changed. I went to my major advisor, Kathy Moran. She wrote a note, so I finally got the grade changed to a "C-." My grades for the fall semester were a "Pass" from an independent course, a "B" from Ms. Christian's course, and a "C-" from the History of Africa course. I saw my professor from that class at the Y in October of 2007, but she didn't recognize me.

In the spring of 1999 I enjoyed my Introduction to History course taught by Professor Litwack. Professor Litwack's course was so popular that it had to be held in Wheeler Auditorium, which seats over seven hundred people. Every seat was filled. Two pages of the schedule of classes were filled with discussion sections held by the GSIs. The course was mostly taken by freshmen whose major was going to be history. In class we read excerpts from *MultiAmerica: Essays on Cultural Wars and Cultural Peace* edited by Ishmael Reed. I have an essay in there called "Being Mixed in America," but it wasn't part of the assignment.

In his class I had first heard of the Spanish-American War and the Philippine-American War in *The United States Becoming a World Power: Volume II* that Professor Litwack co-authored with Winthrop D. Jordan. That was our main textbook. I learned that the Spanish-American War was begun because Spain had rejected the Cubans' demands to emancipate slaves and for self-government. The more I thought about it the more I thought about how ridiculous it was that I went to an expensive middle school and high school that were all about college preparation, but it wasn't until Cal where I studied "the splendid war."

The course was filled with a mix of students from the radical right all the way to the radical left, and they were of many races, religions and backgrounds. Usually the class praised Professor Litwack for his point of view, but when he criticized Ronald Reagan there was complete silence and shock that went through the classroom. But the students got over it because after his last lecture he got a standing ovation. I was one of three

African-American students in the class. My two good friends were white and Chinese-American and the three of us often were horrified by the comments some of the students made, such as the Holocaust in Europe did not happen. When the Ethnic Studies department was being pushed back, the comments got worse because the lack of information made the students voice the stereotypes they hear from home, from the media, and from the White Power curriculum.

When I went to my first discussion section, where I only stayed for two weeks, I was disturbed by the attitude of students. To make up time during the first discussion section, since class didn't start until the next day, the GSI asked us what we felt about the Bill Clinton scandal. Since no one volunteered he called out my name. I said that Clinton was set up because Congress, which was made of Republicans, didn't like his politics. The students wouldn't let me finish what I had to say without being defensive. The harassment had a good result, however. It taught me to hold my ground without getting emotional. A year before I wouldn't have been able to do that.

After the second discussion the following Tuesday, I decided to change sections after I dealt with a young, arrogant and racist English girl who had transferred into our discussion group. She was one of the freshmen students. She said that genocide was the best thing for Native Americans because they were "violent and disobedient." Then she said that slavery was benign and that Africans and African-Americans were "barbaric and inferior." She also said that what the Nazis did wasn't that bad. Then I told her that British people need to get over the fact that they lost Africa, the United States and India as territories. With Professor's Litwack's permission I transferred to another discussion section that was held on Thursday afternoons. I liked the GSI who ran this discussion section and I didn't have any problems with any of the students.

I took an American Studies class taught by writer and professors Gerald Vizenor and Richard Hutson, husband of the head of the American Studies department, Kathy Moran. Professor Moran was one of those responsible for my success at Cal. She had infinite patience and always considered my point of view when it came to my conflict with those who broke the law by not giving me my accommodations.

I found that there were a lot of things that I didn't know about, including the American Indian Movement of the 1960s and '70s, which was very similar to the Civil Rights Movement. A few Native Americans who wanted to promote the traditional ways of life founded the Movement in Minnesota in 1968 to raise questions about the lack of legal services and to bring up charges of treaty violations by the U.S. government. They used the word "genocide" to describe the actions towards Native Americans. In class we read *Ranch Life and the Hunting Trail* by Theodore Roosevelt. It was a cowboy and Indian type diary of Roosevelt's trip in the West. Not only was there animal cruelty throughout the book but there was also a lot of racism.

> Some of the cowboys are Mexicans, who generally do the actual work well enough, but are not trustworthy; moreover, they are always regarded with extreme disfavor by the Texans in an outfit, among whom the intolerant caste spirit is very strong. Southern-born whites will never work under them, and look down upon all colored or half-caste races. One spring I had with my wagon a Pueblo Indian, an excellent rider and roper, but a drunken worthless, lazy devil; and in the summer of 1886 there was a Sioux half-breed, a quiet, hard-working, faithful fellow, and a mulatto, who was one of the best cow-boy hands in the whole round-up. (Roosevelt, Teddy. *Ranch Life and the Hunting Trail*. Lincoln, Nebraska: University of Nebraska Press, 1983.)

At the time I didn't understand why we were required to read this book, but then I figured out that Professor Vizenor and Professor Hutson were trying to make us understand the thinking of the time. The book was published in 1888.

I didn't have any problems with Vizenor's and Hutson's teaching, *per se*, but I had a hard time on the two midterms that we took. One was in late February and one was in mid-April. In most of my other classes at Cal we had a mid-term in late February or early March and then a paper in mid-April. The questions were not clear to me. I got a "D" on the first midterm. I didn't understand what I had done wrong. The problem was that the GSI didn't give us feedback on what we had done wrong to prepare us for the next midterm. I remember looking over the syllabus and being upset when I found out we had another midterm and a final. Most of the other students were happy because they liked exams instead of papers.

I got a "D" on the second midterm. I was so angry. I went and complained to Professor Vizenor. He said that he would look over the midterm himself. A week later Professor Vizenor took me out into the hallway and told me I had gotten a "D" because I "didn't answer the questions." He wasn't angry or frustrated. He just told me how it was. He seemed calm. That's all that was said. If I were thirty-two instead of twenty-two, I would not have attended class that day because I felt like I was going to lose it. I would have just walked away. Instead, I went back to class and sat in between my two friends. I had tears in my eyes, and I was trying hard to push them away, but they poured out anyway and they wouldn't stop. The class didn't know because my back was turned to everyone. My two friends knew. One was really worried. As I said, I hadn't cried at school or in public since I was in middle school, but that day I couldn't help it. I was beyond angry and frustrated. As I said, I only cry when I am really angry and when other emotions that the anger masks come to the surface. At the time I was angry with Professor Vizenor and Professor Hutson but I should have been angry with the GSI as well because the GSI wasn't doing his job and Professor Vizenor and Professor Hudson weren't supervising him closely enough.

What I was the most angry and frustrated about was that I paid all that money for the school and the GSIs were the ones who gave us the tests and the grades. They were often incompetent and immature. The teachers didn't seem to be supervising the GSIs enough to see how they wrote and graded the tests or to see how poorly some of them treated the students. When I was teaching that one semester at Merritt College in the fall of 2005, six and a half years after this course, I saw what the problem was. I wasn't getting much help from my mentor. I felt lost and scared because I didn't know what I was doing. I didn't know how to grade a paper or make comments or corrections on papers. I became an incompetent teacher. Dr. Foster and my students were frustrated with me and I with them. I realize now that the young man that I had for a GSI directed his anger towards us. Just like I felt lost and scared at Merritt, he probably felt lost and scared.

Right before I turned twenty-two in late February of 1999, I decided to attend an Affirmative Action rally on the spur of the moment. I made a speech saying that the Proposition 209, the measure ending Affirmative Action in California, favored white women, who can afford good schools and Advanced Placement courses. I also said that unlike kids in the inner city, people who live in the suburbs could send their kids to schools that aren't crowded. The media are among those institutions that influence the ignorance about the plight of black students—especially black boys. Typical was the sensational reporting of test scores by Katy Murphy in *The Oakland Tribune* (August 15, 2008.) The title of the article was "Oakland's Test Scores Rising." In order to embarrass African-Americans and Latinos, the front age showed six smiling Asian-Americans.

Left out of the model minority stereotype were South Asian-American students, Cambodians and others who struggle with test scores as much as blacks and Latinos.

Though Latinos and blacks, in 2001, had reading scores that were about the same, blacks were singled out by a spokesperson from the Oakland Unified School District's assessment office. Ms. Murphy did nothing to draw his attention to the scores of the Latinos, whose test scores were about the same and whose population percentages in Oakland are the same 36 per cent. The white students' test scores in Oakland were 82 per cent. Ms. Murphy's "analysis" was anything but that and the emphasis on the failure of black students was typical of a newspaper that, daily, associates blacks almost exclusively with crime. This sells papers. Why wasn't this "education editor" familiar with a report from *Education Week*? Citing this report might have introduced more nuances to her article. The Schott Foundation for Public Education published a result that was reported on by Christina A. Samuels. It listed causes for the low reading skills of African-American boys that were ignored by Ms. Murphy. Michael Holzman, a research consultant for the foundation, said, "Schools enrolling large numbers of black male students are not as good as schools with a large population of white students. The teachers are not as experienced and effective, the schools lack resources, and the curriculum is not as challenging. Non-black students enrolled at such schools, he said, also did not graduate at the same rate as their counterparts in schools that had fewer black students." It doesn't occur to Ms. Murphy that black and Latino students might be the victims of a new form of racism: Latté Racism. The racism of the gentrifiers. Her favorite candidate, Jody London, obviously ran a platform that promised with a wink and a nod that such students would be kept out of the white-segregated school, Chabot Elementary School. After the election, Ms. London's favorite school received 17 million dollars of the taxpayers' money to fix the portables, while the schools attended by black and Latino students struggled to buy textbooks. My friend Eva, who said that even though Berkeley High School was integrated (since it is the only public high school in Berkeley) students of color were discouraged to attend Advanced Placement (AP) courses. The counselors tell them, "Are you sure you want to take these AP courses? They're very hard."

Another reason why we need Affirmative Action is because of the racism that one hears in the classroom mostly from classmates, but also from GSIs and professors. I have heard many racist comments from classmates as well as from some of my friends. I heard a student say in a class that when she went to a high school in Rhode Island, "unqualified" minorities took the place of "qualified" white high school seniors. Another student replied, "It's because of people like her that we need Affirmative Action."

It isn't just white people who say these hurtful things. I heard through a friend that a student in one of his classes said, "Somebody had to pick the cotton." The speaker was a Chinese-American. Of course, no one in the class knew a bit about Chinese or black history to challenge him on that very nasty remark. If I were in the class, I would tell him, "Be careful what you say, because someone might tell you, 'Somebody had to build the railroads.'" Cheap Chinese labor was used to build the railroads in the West. The Chinese workers were often lynched and even subjected to massacres.

Through BAMN (By Any Means Necessary) I met Heather, Hoku, Dorothy, and Ronald. Through them I met Mark, Yvette, Gana, Mariah,

Tania, Vincent, Richard, Sheree, Doug and Andrea. Speaking at the rally introduced me to new friends. In March and April, I helped them leaflet. Our candidates ran for University Senate. They lost.

In March and April, I traveled with Heather and Hoku to Lowell High School in San Francisco. There was a lawsuit from three Chinese-American families claiming that their children were being denied enrollment because of race-based preferences. Yet, as my father pointed out, the Chinese-American Democratic Club supported Affirmative Action and Chinese-American contractors in San Francisco benefitted from the measure. Lowell High School chooses students by their test scores. I found out from Heather that three-quarters of the school was Chinese-American, and that there were only thirty-four black students out of 864 students. During the next year there were only going to be eight black freshmen entering the campus.

There was an African-American girl at Lowell who was racist towards African-Americans. I didn't know what event in her history made her so racist. Somebody must have done her wrong. She was talking about how people should have a choice of where to send their children, and how they have a responsibility to find a school that suits the needs of their children. Lowell High School was in an upper-class neighborhood near San Francisco State called the Sunset District. I agree with her that students should have an option to go outside of their neighborhood to go to school, yet she went about it the wrong way.

I told this girl that not everyone has a choice of where to go to school because of the problem of the good schools being too expensive, the standardized tests that one has to take and do well on in order to get in and the fact that most schools are chosen by the district because of the neighborhoods they live in. There is a lot of paperwork involved in transferring kids into a school outside of their neighborhood. I had to go through that several times. I was angry with her. She told me, "I'm just playing the devil's advocate." Hoku and Heather told me that she was just confused.

I also went with them to the old federal courthouse in San Francisco's Civic Center, which is about to be torn down. The judge was an old white conservative. He was chubby, and had round blue eyes and a red face. He was almost deaf and he was really slow. He already had his mind made up. He wanted to resegregate the high schools in San Francisco. The kids who attended middle school and high school in San Francisco spoke up and were very articulate. They told the judge that the school hadn't told them about the lawsuit and that they were upset about the lack of communication. Before we went inside, we rallied outside the courthouse.

In March of 1999, we went to the UC Regents meeting at UC San Francisco. Ward Connerly was there, as well as our former Democratic governor Gray Davis. A couple of my friends attacked Ward Connerly verbally. The speech I had made at the Affirmative Action rally gave me confidence. During the Regents' meeting I rose and addressed the Regents, Connerly, and Governor Davis. I asked, "How can a student get a 4.0 GPA if they have to sit on the floor because of inadequate classroom space?" He just sat there and laughed. My exchange with him was carried on local television.

When I turned thirty, I began to understand where the students who were against Affirmative Action were coming from, even though I still feel that Affirmative Action is needed. When I worked at the Center for Independent Living in Berkeley from November 2006 through October 2007 the executive director, Mrs. Garrett, a middle-aged white woman from Oklahoma City, hired an African-American woman who didn't have the qualifications for working with disabled people, particularly those with non-apparent disabilities. The management and staff weren't given the proper ergonomic equipment and some had to go on medical leave because their back problems got worse like mine due to the working conditions, an odd stance for an organization that raises funds on the basis of their work on behalf of the disabled. I remember my primary care physician calling her an "idiot." When one employee, a good friend of mine, went on medical leave for severe back pain, she was terminated. I was told that this woman who was responsible for this situation was hired because she was African-American and they needed to fill their quotas.

I ended the spring of 1999 with a "C+" in American Studies and "A-" in American History.

In the fall of 1999, I started my second year at UC Berkeley. It was much different than the fall of 1998. I enrolled earlier than I had the previous year, so I got the classes I wanted. I was able to enroll earlier since I was a continuing student. I knew the school, I had a DSP counselor and I had a lot of friends. I didn't feel scared and alone.

I took a course called U.S. Imperialism. The students were mostly Filipino, Cuban and Puerto Rican. My professor was Cuban-American. We read Teddy Roosevelt in this class, too. We also read books by Cubans and Filipinos, but they were upper-class writers and they held views that were against their own people. Therefore, the reading wasn't very balanced. I, as well as two of my friends, Barbara who was Filipina, and Dalisai, who was Puerto Rican, were upset about this. I remember one young Puerto Rican man who said to us sarcastically, "Well why don't *you* make the reading list then?"

Our professor loved Teddy Roosevelt. I had asked him why we were reading Teddy Roosevelt when the goal of the class was to read the points of view of the islanders, whose homelands were annexed by America, according to his syllabus. His response to me was calling Theodore Roosevelt a "great intellectual." I looked around at my classmates and none of them were happy with his remark.

In his class we were required to read *Tarzan* by Edgar Rice Burroughs and also watch the original *Tarzan* movie filmed in 1918. A famous Olympic swimmer, Elmo Lincoln, played the role of "Tarzan." I had never seen the original version of *Tarzan* nor had I read the book. The 1999 Disney version of Tarzan that I saw in the theatres during the summer with longtime friend Elaine Overstreet was much more benign, even for a Disney movie. In the book, there was a Mammy figure named Ezmeralda who traveled with Jane and her father to Africa from Maryland. My professor had a son in the Oakland public schools where reading *Tarzan* had become a requirement. This was someone's idea of an introduction to African history and culture. I guess this means that the public school system in Oakland must want to tell black kids to be ashamed of their African heritage and to be more like Jane and Tarzan.

In the beginning of the book, an ape rapes and kills Tarzan's human mother and kills his human father. My father has made me aware of how to interpret movies and books such as this. Edgar Rice Burroughs, the author of this book, wrote it based on his fantasies of Africa. The GSI asked us during our discussion section what we thought the author was thinking when he wrote this. I said that the author was thinking that the ape was a black man trying to rape and kill a white woman. This theme has been an American obsession since the Reconstruction era. The book was published in 1912, three years before D. W. Griffith's film *Birth of a Nation* came out. I also thought that the ape abandoned Tarzan because Burroughs was trying to say that all black fathers abandon their children. This is another obsession and theme, even to this day. Surprisingly, a lot of the class agreed with me. The GSI turned red. He was a Latino. I was the only black person in the class.

My mother, Carla Blank, taught one of my other classes, Interdisciplinary Studies. It was a Twentieth Century Art course. During my stay at Cal, she, my father, Professor Christian and Professor Litwack were the only four teachers at Cal who encouraged multiculturalism in their classrooms. Mom had us read manifestos by writers such as Leslie Marmon Silko, Frank Chin and Alain Locke. They accused white authors and movie directors, who wrote about Native Americans, Asian-Americans and African-Americans, of thinking that they could understand what it was like to be a member of these cultures just like the 2005 movie, written by a white man, *Memoirs of a Geisha*, where they had Chinese actresses instead of Japanese actresses play the parts. The authors also accused them of thinking they knew more about these cultures than the members of these cultures knew about themselves. The white authors and movie directors had many stereotypes of these cultures, especially of women, that the manifestoes also used. She addressed these issues in her own book *Rediscovering America: The Making of Multicultural America, 1900–2000* published in 2003 by Three Rivers Press.

My mother also invited artists, writers and scholars to visit her class. They were people such as the late Andrew Hope, a Tlingit Indian, and Yoruba professor Adebisi Aromolaran from Nigeria. They talked about life in Alaska and Nigeria as well as slavery and treaties. One young white woman asked if African-Americans would be able to find their roots in Africa. Ade said that since African-Americans were mixed, they wouldn't be able to. She also showed us films and art by many different cultures. We saw a film of Alvin Ailey's *Revelations,* films of Suzushi Hanayagi, her longtime friend and collaborator, and films of many other dancers. Suzushi worked with stage director Robert Wilson, who used some of Mom and Suzushi's earlier source materials in "The Forest." We also saw artwork by many different artists as well, such as Louise Nevelson who had an exhibit at the De Young Museum in the fall of 2007. This was one of the few exhibits where her entire collection had been put on public display. The final exam was fun but hard. It was an essay and we were able to look at images and discuss our points-of-view towards things like the manifestos and artwork. I took my final at home before anyone else. I had one good friend in the course. Both of us were laughing when my mom told the students, "Just because I show a video in class doesn't mean the class is over."

Dad was his usual amusing self in his class. A student I knew about from the people in BAMN, who called himself "White Mike" had criticized Dad's teaching style in his English Creative Writing course. To put us in our place Dad said, "Now I know any one of you can teach the class better than me but they hired me." The class reacted in silence except for me. I was laughing. A friend of mine named Michael asked another friend of mine named Benedict, "Who pissed him off?" and she replied, "I don't know."

I was worried that I wouldn't be able to take the criticism from my fellow classmates. I took it so well that even my father was surprised. I wrote a poem about Teddy Roosevelt. The assignment was to write from the point of view of the opposite sex. I wrote a poem about who Teddy Roosevelt really was using his voice in a dramatic monologue because most Americans think that he was a great guy. He hated Indians and thought black people were inferior. A few of my fellow classmates were appalled that I would write a poem questioning the career of this icon. They said that I was bashing him. I told them that this was the point of my poem. One of my classmates told me that he didn't care about Teddy Roosevelt. A few of the other classmates agreed. This young man said that it was almost the year 2000 and that Roosevelt was president during the beginning of the last century. I said that if he lived in the Philippines, Cuba, Hawaii, or Puerto Rico, he would care because he would still be living the effects of Roosevelt's presidency. The U.S. still does military testing on those islands. He didn't know what to say.

I had quite a few friends in that class. I hung with them in between classes. We had lunch together. I wrote a lot of new poems. The fall semester went by really quickly, and it was already time for finals. I aced them all. I had a great six weeks off and then it was time for the spring of 2000.

The spring of 2000 was a disappointment. My classes were disappointing not only because of the teachers, but because the classes didn't go as planned. I somewhat enjoyed my Landscapes in the Bay Area course. Not the lectures, but the field trips. Our assignment was to write about any building that we discussed in class or had seen. I went on trips to the Embarcadero and Chinatown in San Francisco, San Francisco's Civic Center and West Oakland. The teacher was bigoted though. The beginning of the course was the history of Bay Area Indians. She told us that the Indians went through a recession not genocide. She also said that segregated neighborhoods were a sign of "racial harmony." The GSI was a hyperactive woman. I thought I was hyper until I met her. I suspected she might have ADHD. She also seemed to go off-topic a lot, a behavior I share since I also have ADHD.

I chose to write my paper on San Francisco's City Hall. I went on a tour of the exterior of the building. I visited the South Light Court, the North Light Court, the basement, the rotunda, the Board of Supervisors' Chambers (Room 258) and the Mayor's office (Room 200, which is many little rooms). Willie Brown had just been re-elected for his second term. I talked about the architecture, structural engineering and the history of the building, as well as the influence of the City Beautiful Movement, a movement that was designed to make San Francisco resemble a European city like Paris. The movement took hold after the 1906 earthquake. I sent the paper to Willie Brown. He was so impressed with it that he sent me a signed note, which I found on my bed when I returned from England on

July 12, 2000. He sent my paper on to architect Tony Irons, who designed the post-1989 earthquake City Hall. I got an "A-" on the paper.

I also took a course with Robert Allen, author of *Port Chicago*, which was a big disappointment. The class I mean. What started my anger towards him and the GSI was our first multiple-choice test. I thought I had done well on the test. But when I got it back I was really angry. I had failed. I went to talk to him about it and his reply was, "Why did you think you passed? You chose the wrong answers to each question." He was upset when he said this. My confidence was shot. I went to someone else for a second opinion. They agreed with him. Not only was I angry because I had lost in the conflict but because my confidence was gone. My grades reflected my anger.

The incident that was the final straw was when one of his graduate student assistants came to talk to the class. This guy was a right-wing Jew. He thought he would be accepted as white because he was very pale, had blonde hair and blue eyes. He even said that Jewish people were white. I corrected him, saying that most Jews are semitic and many have ancestors from Asia and Africa and asked why they had been gassed throughout Europe if they were considered white. He got defensive and cussed me out in front of the class because he really didn't have an answer to that question. Then he started making JAP (Jewish American Princess) jokes and laughing. I remember how some of them went like:

1) Why do Jews have such big noses?

   Because the air is free.

2) What do you get if you cross a Jew with a Gypsy?

   A chain of empty retail stores.

3) How did they know that Jesus was Jewish?

   Because he lived at home until he was thirty, he went into his father's business, his mother thought he was God, and he thought his mother was a virgin.

4) What does a Jewish American Princess make for lunch?

   Reservations.

The black students thought it was funny but no one else did. Therefore, I felt they had no room to accuse white people of being racist. In the class, there was an African-American girl who fit the stereotype of the angry black female. She also thought the incident was funny. She was part of this group that was like the colored Ku Klux Klan. These were young people of color who held hatred towards people with mixed blood and believed that there should be a law against interracial marriage, yet these people were probably mixed as well. A young Filipina friend of hers understood my anger. She used to be part of the group. I told her if she looked at the history of the Philippines she would see that Filipinos are a mixture of Spanish and Chinese as well as Filipino, and Camille, the girl who I got into the fight with, was probably mixed with European and Native American as well as black. This young woman was trying to tell me not to take it personally. Anyway, Camille and me almost got into a physical confrontation. What stopped me from engaging her was when my friend from BAMN, a young man mixed with Nigerian, Filipino and white, and who was gay to the core, got in between the two of us.

I had an appointment to see my professor who gave me an angry lecture and then told me to apologize to the GSI for questioning him and interrupting him in front of the class. That was on a Thursday. The following Tuesday this professor spoke to me as if nothing had happened. I wasn't quick to forgive, so I pretended like he wasn't there. I was upset. I chose not to interact with him as the GSI came around to each small group. It worked, even though he talked to the group as a whole. I'm still angry about that incident. Later on Dad told the chair of the African-American Studies Department, Dr. Percy Hintzen, "There is a young man who is making anti-semitic comments in Professor Allen's course and I know that the African American Studies budget is up for review." Dr. Hintzen's reply was, "I get to it! I get to it!" I never apologized to the young man because I felt there was nothing to apologize about.

I didn't like my own GSI for that class, either. Her logic escaped me. She said that she didn't have any trouble being biracial because people thought she was black. I told her that may be true for her, but it isn't for someone like me who is an obvious mixture of everything. I told her I got racist treatment from both white people and black people. She quickly changed the subject.

She also said that Jewish people were white. "My mother is a white woman," she said on several occasions. There was a lot of overbearing and insolence on her part. She often ignored me when I wanted to make a comment. One day I got angry with her about her attitude. After class, I went up to her and tried to speak to her. She still ignored me. After that we didn't speak to each other.

I survived the spring 2000 semester and in March or April I received a letter stating that I was going to be a senior in the fall. I was so happy. I took my final exams early and then went to England for two and half months.

CHAPTER TEN

My Senior Year In College

I SPENT A MAJORITY OF THE SUMMER OF 2000 AT THE UNIVERSITY of Luton, England studying Creative Writing with Professor Lauri Ramey and Religious Studies with her husband Professor Marty Ramey. Dad had met Lauri and Marty at Hampton University in Virginia in the spring of 1999. I was supposed to visit them in the fall of 1999 at Hampton, the week Hurricane Floyd hit, but at the last minute they moved to Luton, a small town north of London. Marty was a minister at a white Hampton church. He said that the church fired him because he had invited my father to show a film of his, *Gethsemane Park: a Gospera*, an unorthodox libretto about the arrest of Jesus of Nazareth by Roman soldiers. In Dad's version, Judas is the hero and Lazarus complains about being brought back from the dead. Composer Carman Moore wrote the music. I arrived in Luton on May 7, 2000 and returned to Oakland on July 12, 2000. I was hoping to make a lot of friends but it was hard because the semester ended soon after I got there and the students had left. I didn't stay with Lauri and Marty because there was no room in their home and they were going to move. I stayed with an older woman and her twenty-three-year-old son. This wasn't my first trip to England. I had gone with my parents in March of 1989 where I traveled to London, Nottingham and Canterbury. That was my twelfth birthday present.

I traveled to London with one young woman named Tammy. She was British born but her mother was Jamaican and her father Dominican. She had relatives in the United Sates and the Caribbean. I stayed with her for a few days in the middle of June in West London. I really enjoyed her and her mother. I also met her neighbors, who were an elderly German couple. They were really nice and I remember discussing my trips to Germany with them. Tammy took me to Saint Paul's Cathedral and the Natural History Museum in central London. I had wanted to go to

Saint Paul's since I had seen the movie *Mary Poppins*. Christopher Wren designed Saint Paul's Cathedral. I also have enjoyed studying natural history, which is why I wanted to go to the Natural History Museum. I have been to the American Museum of Natural History in New York many times. I have also visited natural history museums in San Francisco, Los Angeles, Seattle, Pittsburgh, Cambridge in Massachusetts, and Frankfurt, Germany.

I made friends at the University Church, even though I didn't agree with their idea of traveling to Africa and South America to convert Africans and Indians. While in England, I had a dream about Jesus and the apostles. They were gathered at La Loma Park in the Berkeley Hills overlooking the San Francisco Bay. In the dream, he was crucified in the park.

The university was small compared to U.C. Berkeley, but it was diverse. The faculty and staff treated me with open arms. The town however, was very white, mostly full of poor white people. It was very provincial and the people were full of prejudices. My landlady was one of them. She believed that all children should learn to speak at a certain age and if they didn't, there was something wrong with them. She felt that all disabled people were retarded, no matter what their disabilities were. She didn't believe in interracial marriages and she was anti-Semitic and anti-Catholic. Her son threatened to beat up the Indian neighbors. This landlady didn't like anyone who wasn't an older rich white Anglo-Saxon Protestant.

Right after I entered my senior year I decided to look at graduate schools. I applied to the Teaching Cultural Program at the University of San Francisco in the middle of the fall, a Jesuit school in the city's Inner Richmond district. If I had gone there I would have been teaching from nine to five Monday through Friday and taking classes from six to eight on Tuesdays, Wednesdays and Thursdays. I found out about it through Herb Kohl, the program director. He is a longtime friend of my parents. The off-campus housing was ridiculously overpriced thanks to gentrification. My dad suggested staying at the YWCA, but there weren't any residential Ys in San Francisco. It wound up being a problem.

I was thinking about maybe going to New College, which is also in San Francisco, or San Francisco State. They had teaching credential programs during the day. I could have commuted on BART, and I knew where the school was. Plus it was learning disabled friendly. My friends in BAMN also suggested UC Berkeley's Education department, which was an AC Transit bus ride away. A few of them taught at the Oakland Public Schools and they could set me up for student teaching.

In terms of studying, I did pretty well. I succeeded in writing my Senior Thesis. Professor Hall was one of the best teachers I had at Cal. She is Professor Vizenor's wife. The course was set up in an organized fashion, which helped my research process. She had divided each section by weeks. For instance, for the first two weeks of classes we had to choose our topics. My topic was about the education of African-Americans and disabled people. Throughout September, we did research and by early October we took library research classes. The first draft was due November 1, 2000. By November 1, 2000 I had more work done than any of the other students. Twenty-five out of thirty pages were written. Professor Hall was impressed. It wasn't due until December 6, 2000. I revised it during the next month. I had it copied and bound to make it look nice. Dad was impressed. He had never seen it until then. He said that I sounded like a scholar. Since the class had structure, I did well.

I took an African-American music course with my friend Andrea. I forgot the name of the course. That was one of the hardest courses I took at Cal. It should have been a graduate level course. A person needed to have studied music for at least ten years and also needed to take a lot of African history courses. The only really interesting thing for me about the course was when some musicians from West Africa came. We went to Herbst Hall where there were huge pipe organs. Anyway, I got to play the Ganqonqui, a set of bells from West Africa. I demonstrated how to play them in front of the entire class. After that other instruments came in and then we danced.

I got an "F" on the first midterm. Not a lot of people did well. Andrea even said she had a panic attack during that midterm. Right around Thanksgiving Andrea, her boyfriend Doug, their friend, Fele, and I went to talk to Professor Olly Wilson. We explained to him the nature of my disability, so he told me that I could retake the midterm. He was among those teachers who were sympathetic to the needs of learning disabled students. My dad says that it's because Professor Wilson is a composer and that many great artists were probably learning disabled like Beethoven, Bud Powell and Thelonious Monk. Andrea helped me out a lot between Thanksgiving and the make-up midterm. I wound up getting a "B-." In between then and the final Andrea and I studied hard together. Then we took the final. We celebrated by eating vanilla frozen yogurt with M&Ms.

I had a boyfriend for a couple of months. I had met him at Laney in the fall of 1996. Between then and the spring of 1998, he and I were good friends. He had an accident and I left Laney in the spring of 1998. I hadn't seen him again until 2000. He was really strange. He kept a lot of secrets from me about his personal life that I needed to know. He told me that he didn't want me wearing skirts anymore because that would make other men look at me. I told him if he felt that way perhaps I should cover myself up completely like the women in the Middle East do. Between the middle of October and the middle of November I got sick with two colds and I wasn't eating much. When I became healthy I began to eat more since my body was lacking nutrition. He told me that I was "binge eating" and that I looked like I was gaining weight. Since my appearance is very important to me, anybody who puts down my appearance has to go.

He also wanted to get married and have kids. I told him that wouldn't be possible since I thought I would be in graduate school. He was calling me his "fiancée" and he wanted to get engaged. I told him that I wasn't ready for commitment and that I don't have the finances for all of this. I also told him that I don't have time for kids because I can't breast feed a baby when I take night classes and I can't be up all night with a baby. I also couldn't afford formula, diapers, clothes, the crib, the changing table, the car seat, the stroller and all of the other baby needs. I also wasn't willing to give up my virginity. He got upset and said that I was "too busy." I told him I'm not giving up my life for him. Of course I was busy.

By December 4, 2000, two days before I turned in my thesis, I was tired of him. So I told him how I felt and then I told him it was time to break it off. My friends were speechless. Andrea, Doug, Vincent, Ronald and Laura were there. He left. I only ran into him a couple of times after that but we didn't talk. He also paged me. The semester ended well however, because I got an "A" on my thesis, my second "A" from UC Berkeley. That was the hardest assignment I had at Cal.

The spring of 2001 felt long and slow. I was ready to leave college and start working. I needed a break from school. I was mostly tired of the dormitory/co-op I was in. I hadn't been eating or sleeping well since I began living in the dormitories starting in the fall of 1998. I tried to only stay there during my sleeping hours. I got frequent colds. I was also tired of the filthy bathrooms. I had to share the bathroom with men and women who obviously had maids in their homes growing up because they did not pick up after themselves. I also got tired of all of the noise. The walls were so thin that I could hear what people were doing in their rooms. One time, I woke up to go to the bathroom and I heard two people having sex. I feel that sex is a private thing, meaning it should not be seen or heard by others. The supervisor did nothing to stop this when I complained that this was going on throughout the night.

I was upset with my dorm mates all of the time. People would run up and down the hallways laughing and talking loud. Since this was a dorm for upper classmen, I felt that they were too old to be fooling around like this. I couldn't study or sleep. I kept the TV on all night. It was either too cold or too hot in the room. When I entered Mills for graduate school in the fall of 2003, I made sure that I didn't have to stay in the dorms. I found out that I was healthier and happier. I ate and slept better, and my GPA was a 3.55 instead of a 2.89.

I later found out that the Barrows House dormitories/co-op got a one out of ten approval rating on everything from security to appearance (ten being the best and one being the worst) when I researched it online in early 2008. This is one of the reviews I found.

"This rooming house is not being cleaned often enough given the number of people who live there. The bathrooms often smell and there are excrements floating in the toilets. The toilets are often jammed. The landlord is completely uncooperative as far as doing any repairs or cleaning the house. The managers are total assholes."

Another review I found said:

"Very dirty. Things disappear if left in common areas even briefly. Landlord and managers are ———-s. Stay away!"

Both reviews were found on www.apartmentratings.com/rate/CA-Berkeley-Barrows-House.html. This was my experience. When we took our complaints to the manager, he never responded. One time, he changed the security code on the door without telling us and he didn't fix the pay phone or our phones when a storm knocked the power out. He let the students run around, smoke and bring their boyfriends or girlfriends over.

I was upset about two out of my three courses. I was really upset about the fact that the field course I was going to take was cancelled, so I entered the semester angry about that. It would have given me some important skills for teaching. I was also tired of BAMN. They became anti-Semitic. One instance, when the Palestinian students staged a protest against the Israeli Jews, one of the BAMN members participated. The rest of them stayed at the table. They pressured me to participate in the march, but I refused saying that I didn't want to be involved in something that was anti-Semitic. Their reply was, "It's not anti-Semitic. It is anti-Zionist." After that I felt some tension between BAMN and myself. I began to gradually push them away from me. BAMN didn't support my fight to bring back tutoring to the disabled students' program. I got into a bad argument with Andrea and Doug. I was having a bad case of senioritis.

I found out that by the end of the fall of 2000 I had enough units to graduate in May of 2001, thanks to the summer in England at Luton College (and let me tell you, it took many months to get my transcripts from them.) I was quite excited. There was a class called "the Urban Community" that was under the City Planning department. I had always been interested in transportation and how cities are built. Since I was a child I have been interested in buildings, especially old European style buildings like San Francisco City Hall.

The course was taught by a black man, who had been born in Jamaica and raised in Toronto. He also lived in New York, but back then, he was living in San Francisco with his wife and son who was born three weeks into the semester. There were a lot of immigrants as well as people from all over the country in the class. There were a few people born in California, but mostly from southern California.

The class focused on things such as the American Dream, immigration, multiculturalism, racism, neighborhoods, urban renewal, gentrification, streets, suburbs and transportation. The material was very interesting, but it was hard to find liberals and radical writing on the reading list. There were a lot of right-wing students. They weren't only white. They were Asian and black as well. They said that multiculturalism was racist because "it looked at people's differences instead of their similarities." I explained that as long as there was racism there needed to be multiculturalism. Then they told me that multiculturalism would lead to self-segregation. I stated that multiculturalism was formed because it was a way for people to learn their history and culture. They wouldn't learn it in the schools. I also said it was important because it would build people's self-esteem. I talked a little about the Universal Negro Improvement Association formed by Marcus Garvey, the National Association for the Advancement of Colored People formed by W.E.B. Du Bois, Walter White and others and the Black Panther Party formed by Bobby Seale and Huey Newton. I also talked about The American Indian Movement, as well as La Raza Unida and NOW. Some of the students nodded but others refused to listen. The professor enabled their behaviors. There was a text written by a Chinese author, who had just moved to San Francisco. The author was deeply racist towards black people. The essay contained nearly every stereotype about black men you could find. Then she wrote, "My son's best friend is black" to justify the behavior. Racism 101.

Most of the students in the class were prejudiced towards the inner city. They grew up in the suburbs. I am prejudiced towards the suburbs because I have had bad experiences out there. For instance, my friend Heather lives in Fremont. I visited her one time between Christmas of

1998 and New Year's of 1999. It is colder in Fremont than it is in Oakland during the winter, so I had on a beanie cap, a puff jacket, some pants and sneakers. We went to some mall out there. An older white woman saw me and in fear pulled her two granddaughters towards her. Another time, I visited Heather in the summer of 1996 and we went out to Pleasanton to a mall and people in the store followed me. We have Pakistani friends who live in the Fremont hills. Wajahat Ali, a former student of Dad and a young playwright and lawyer, lives with his parents and grandmother and we occasionally go down there to visit them. Usually we are there in the daytime, but one time we went out there at night. It gets very dark at night. Luckily, we had the GPS so we wouldn't get lost. Dad said that Fremont is the kind of town he wouldn't want to be in after sunset. I found out Fremont was a "sundown town" in James Loewen's book *Sundown Towns*, a bad place to be after a certain time of day if you were black. That does not surprise me. In the summer of 1994, there was a cross-burning in Fremont and then in the fall of 2000 a high school was attacked with anti-Semitic vandalism with a swastika and "die Jew" spray-painted on the wall.

One young woman wrote about crime in the inner city. She said that crime was absent from the suburbs and that she wouldn't live in a city like Oakland, San Francisco or San Jose because of gangs. Yet one study reports that the abuse of women in the suburbs is widespread. White women are reluctant to discuss it. A young Chinese-American man agreed. He grew up in Skokie, Illinois, a suburb of Chicago. The professor asked him, "Well didn't the Nazis march down the street in Skokie?" He said they did, but he would rather live there than in Chicago. My response was the difference between crime in the inner city and in the suburbs was that inner city crime was random. I also asked them "Where are all the school shootings taking place? Do they take place in the city?" In the suburbs, hate crimes are aimed at a particular group of people like Mexicans, Jews or blacks. Beverly Louw, a principal at Lancaster High School, said:

> The most serious problems I ever had are with white supremacists. I'd take any black gang or Hispanic gang or Asian gang over white

supremacists. They appear to have absolutely no conscience. Our strategies for working with gang kids don't work with white-supremacist kids. They won't be part of a discussion group or counseling. It's almost like a religion or something. (*The New Yorker*, June 5, 2008.)

Those were just a few of the examples I heard in this class. The teacher said little to oppose these arguments. At our last discussion section, the GSI asked us who wanted to take the course and who had to take the course. It was an American Cultures course. A young man from Russia said that he was a physics major and didn't need a course on multiculturalism. A young woman from Orange County said that she learned all that she needed about other cultures in high school. After listening to the ignorance in class, I was wondering how they could have been able to pass the SATs because they sounded so unintelligent and lacking in intellectual curiosity.

The professor got angry with me because I had trouble understanding the reading material the first time. Even though my reading comprehension has improved a lot throughout the years, it will never be perfect because my disability is permanent. The professor said, "If I could read this chapter while I'm feeding my kid his bottle than you could read this, too." As the semester went on I realized that his arrogance was his hang up, not mine. That was just his nature. He was in his thirties and should have been out of that phase. Some people don't grow out of it.

To replace the education field course that was cancelled, I decided to enroll in an Ethnic Studies course called "Women of Color in the U.S." That didn't work because it was so crowded that people had to sit on the floor. Also the teacher talked in a soft voice. I found a course called "African-Americans in the Industrial Age," (a.k.a. Black Feminist Ideology, which I found out later.) The course covered the post-Reconstruction period to the 1970s. I wanted to take this course because I wanted to learn more about Reconstruction, the Great Migration and the Great Depression. The people in BAMN told me that the course was taught by a great professor. I heard so many people praise her that I decided I just had to take a course from her before I left Cal.

I found something quite odd with this professor. I was wondering why she would shake other people's hands when they made good points, but she wouldn't shake my hand when I made a good point. I knew right away what the problem was. I took it personally at the time even though I shouldn't have. I knew that there was going to be anger and frustration between the two of us, but unfortunately I couldn't drop the course because I needed those three units to graduate.

The first thing that went really wrong was when I got the midterm back. I got an "F." I didn't understand why. I had studied hard for that midterm. I talked to her during her office hours and we decided that I could do a take-home midterm. I found out that she had the usual myths that teachers have about the learning disabled, like my not taking notes as a sign that I wasn't interested in the course. What really angered me was that the professor had us clap for the three people who did the best on the midterm. To compound my problems, I didn't have one of the textbooks. The bookstore didn't have any more copies of one particular book, which title I forget, and the professor didn't order anymore even though I told her they didn't have any. I went to different libraries and bookstores and they didn't carry it. I didn't have the means or the know-how to buy books online. I was very angry because having that book would have made a difference on whether or not I was going to pass the exams and the course. I don't know if anyone else was in that situation because I didn't ask.

The following Monday, I did the take-home midterm and turned it in on Wednesday. I must admit that I wasn't in a good state of mind. It was the Wednesday before spring break. The professor took offense that I wasn't taking notes. If she had read my accommodation letter she would have seen that I needed a note taker. She even announced that I needed a note taker. She decided that she could ridicule me in front of the class, so she said, "You need to do some writing" (which now sounds trivial because teachers have said worse things to me than that and have even called me names, and as it turned out, I had published more than she). Everyone turned and looked at me. I had a flashback to Harriet and Susan's K/1 class at Park School where they would ridicule me in front of the class. I got into a panic attack and I began to hyperventilate and cry. I went to the bathroom and then I called Mom. She told me to talk to Deirdre, my counselor at the Disabled Students' Program. She was a middle-aged Jewish woman who was born in Albuquerque and raised in Tucson.

I left my backpack and Gatorade in the classroom and went to Campbell Hall to talk to Kathy Moran and Jain Hutson. I asked if I would have enough units to graduate if I dropped the course. I was told that I would be three units short, but I could still walk the stage. I would have had to take courses in the summer. Dad thought that I should stay in the course. The professor was also upset that I didn't sit with the rest of the class. The reason I didn't sit with the class was because the rows of tables had the chairs attached to them. My feet weren't able to reach the floor and that aggravated my lower back pain.

Her reader was even worse. We met at a cafe to look over the rough draft of my Marcus Garvey paper, my next project. She reminded me of Amber at John Muir. Her hair, skin and eyes were lighter than mine. I could tell she was frustrated because she wasn't dark-skinned and she felt she had to prove that she was twice as African-American.

The reader first told me that she had to grade forty other papers and that she didn't have the time to work with me. Then she told me that she didn't know how to work with people like me. After that, she would retreat from me when I talked to her.

I worked hard on the Marcus Garvey paper. Garvey was born in Saint Ann Parish, Jamaica and as a young man in Jamaica he founded the Universal Negro Improvement Association in 1914. In 1916 he organized a town hall in New York to bring in support for the UNIA. The organization quickly spread all over the Caribbean and Africa. Garvey, through the UNIA, published the journal *Negro World* where he wrote about his Black Nationalist Ideas. Unlike most civil rights organizations, Garvey felt he had a solution to the problem that African-Americans faced in United States: returning to Africa. While the UNIA was in process, Garvey started the Black Cross Navigation and Trading Company. The agency folded due to financial ruin.

While researching this paper, I even went to Marcus Bookstore, a black-owned bookstore during spring break and bought *Garvey: His Work and Impact* by Rupert Lewis and Patrick Bryan. I worked on it more than I did my other homework. I even worked on it with Dad while I was at home during the weekends.

When I got my paper back three weeks after the due date I found I'd received a "C-." It didn't sink in for a while. It was May 1, 2001. I know because I went to Tower Records and bought Destiny Child's CD *Survivor*, which had just hit the stores that day. I came back to campus and I felt like I was going to lose it, but in a much worse way than I did in the spring of 1999 at my American Studies class. I called up Mom on the pay phone and began to cry. I went into Deirdre's office and she looked shocked. I told her that she gave me a "C-" and Deirdre looked over my paper. She told me some of the things I could improve on, but said I deserved at least an "A-/B+."

Dad was livid and the chair of the African-American Studies, Mr. Hintzen called my professor and talked to her. We made an appointment with her for the following Wednesday. I also found out that the reader graded everyone else's papers but mine. I was a nervous wreck so Dad and I looked over my paper and the take-home midterm. I received a "D" on my second midterm. Dad and I tagged the pages in the textbooks that proved my points. I wrote down the pages where I found evidence in a red-colored pencil. Dad and I found out that there weren't enough critical comments written by her on the paper to justify a "C-." An example would be when I stated that W.E.B. Du Bois held his Pan-African Conference in Paris. She asked me, "Why didn't he hold it in Africa?"

Dad and I talked to her and showed her the evidence that supported my midterm. When I talked about sharecropping in the midterm I had said that black women didn't have time to take care of the house so usually it was chaotic. They spent time in the fields or taking care of other people's children. I had taken that out of a quote. Also she asked me why slaves went into sharecropping. That one's obvious. They didn't have any choice because they signed contracts with their former slave masters that required them to return to conditions that existed before the Civil War.

After that we moved on to the paper. Dad said that the comments she made looked like she had something against Marcus Garvey and not against me. That offended her. He also asked, "Do you need to be a black feminist to pass this class?" The professor was shocked. She said, "No, no, absolutely not." Dad just laughed. She looked like she was going to cry. Mom had said that it wasn't a good idea for Dad to go up there. Dad's response was that he thought it necessary to intervene for me on the university level because as someone who taught at the universities for almost three decades, he knew about the treatment of black and Latino students. Mom told me that I had to fight my own battles. This one I couldn't fight alone. The professor was very nervous. Another professor, her close friend, peeked into her office during our conference about ten times probably to offer her moral support. All Dad said to her was, "I'm tired of you." He asked my professor to produce something she had written. She produced one article attacking Garvey for being a male chauvinist.

At the end of the course, we had to do course evaluations. It was what I called "sweet revenge." I got back at her and her reader. When people finished their evaluations they were talking. I heard a lot of the black women and white women praise her. The black men and the white men didn't have anything to say. I was laughing to myself because I knew that it was payback time. At the end the professor had us clap for her reader. I was the only one who didn't applaud.

Dad told me to study for this final more so than for my other two finals so I could pass the course. I usually don't like to put one teacher in competition with another, but since Professor Litwack taught a similar course and I learned a lot more from him. Professor Litwack was deliberate. He gave me more information, so that I could process it better. Leon Litwack was one of the few professors I had who knew how to deal with disabled students.

Leon Litwack's course was great as usual. It was a course on African-Americans in the Jim Crow era. I did well on the exams and I loved his lectures. I was also happy that there were no discussion sections. The course itself had no problems. The problem in that course was Andrea. In the fall of 2000, when the arthritis in her knee got worse, our friendship began to gradually lose its strength. We were good friends for a year and a half and we often saw each other outside of school.

Our friendship stopped abruptly around the early part of February of 2001 about three weeks before my twenty-fourth birthday. What happened was that Andrea became mean because she was tired, had a bad knee and an upper digestive problem.

One day she really hurt my feelings, which is how my anger towards her started. We went to see an exhibit at the University Art Museum. When the class gathered inside the Pacific Film Archives, I asked Andrea to sit next to me. She said, "No, I want to sit next to my friends," in a rude manner. I felt like she was telling me that I wasn't considered her friend. Mom thought that she wasn't thinking and it came out wrong. I moved further down because I didn't want to sit near her. I sat alone feeling stupid. At the end of the class, she walked down Durant Avenue acting as if I didn't exist. When we got to the intersection of Durant and Telegraph she said "Hi," to me. She wanted to talk to me but I just said "Hi," and walked down Telegraph towards Bancroft to meet with my ADHD brown bag lunch group. I wasn't quick to forgive her.

The incident that really damaged my relationship with Andrea was when Professor Litwack told me that he had to announce to the class that I needed a note taker. Andrea wasn't in class as usual. In the past Andrea took notes for me. After she found out that I got another note taker she began to act cold towards me. I found out later, through Doug, her boyfriend, that she got her feelings hurt because of this. I don't know if she realized that she was part of the problem because she and I didn't interact after this. I had to pry her side of the situation out of her boyfriend, Doug. I felt like if she had a problem she could come to me and talk about it instead of with everybody else. Her crankiness from the pain and illness made her hard to be around. I was burnt out, sleep deprived and tense about getting ready to graduate and wasn't in the mood for her behavior. Now that I have chronic back and nerve pain, I can understand where the constant feelings of anger, frustration, anxiety and fear come from. Mom said I could have handled the matter with Andrea better. Eight years later, I still don't know how.

I ended the semester overtired from taking three finals, graduating and moving out of the dormitory. I hadn't eaten or slept well in a while. I came down with a cold.

CHAPTER ELEVEN

My Graduation from College

G RADUATION DAY, THURSDAY MAY 17, 2001, FINALLY CAME. I didn't sleep because I was so excited. My graduation took place outside at the Greek Theatre designed by John Galen Howard in 1903. It was named after William Randolph Hearst the publisher of the *San Francisco Examiner* and the *New York Journal*. His life story was a source of inspiration for the lead character in Orson Welles' classic film, *Citizen Kane*.

In 1982 the Greek Theatre was registered on the National Register of Historic Places. The theater is used for games, concerts and graduations. It is right down the hill from the Lawrence Hall of Science and the Berkeley National Laboratory.

I waited backstage in the shade for an hour. Then it was finally time to start the ceremony. We sat through Robert Hass' speech. Poet Laureate of the United States, Robert Hass was responsible for my dad being invited to the Library of Congress to read his poetry. Before that, Daniel Hoffman brought him to the Library of Congress. Professor Hoffman was the Poet Laureate in the 1970s. Then it was time to walk the stage. Graduates in my major, American Studies, went first. I was first in line.

The ceremony ended at noon. There was a little reception and then we went to Skates by the Bay for lunch. Skates is located on the Berkeley Marina. We sat down by the window. There were sailboats of many colors on the bay. We could see the San Francisco skyline and Alcatraz. The fog was coming in. Our friend, Gundars Strads, executive director of the Before Columbus Foundation and editor of *California Management Magazine*, published by the Hass School of Business, joined us. I had steak with mashed potatoes and vegetables for lunch. I also had chocolate fudge cake. Gundars told a joke. It went like this, "There were a Catholic, a Jew and a black man who entered Heaven. The Catholic asked God,

'What can I do to get into Heaven?' God said, 'Spell God.' The Catholic said, 'That's easy. G-O-D.' The Jew asked the same question. God said, 'Spell God.' The Jew said, 'That's easy. G-O-D.' The black man asked, 'How can I get into Heaven?' God said, 'Spell Albuquerque.'" The point of that joke is that black, Latino, South Asian, Southeast Asian, poor, gay and lesbian and disabled students have to work extra hard to make it into society. That's where I got the name for this book.

I found out that I received a "D" in my "African-Americans in the Industrial Age" course, a "B" in Professor Litwack's course and a "C" in my African-Americans in the Industrial Age class. I wasn't too upset; I just graduated and that was all that mattered. I was happy that I survived Professor Taylor's class and that I didn't have to deal with BAMN, Andrea or the dormitories anymore.

For my participation in BAMN I received an admonishment from the campus police that lasted five years, which was odd because I was going to graduate that semester. I had gotten that letter because they thought I had participated in the March rally on the steps of Sproul Hall, even though I was taking a midterm for my City Planning course. Because of a demonstration of high school students, organized by BAMN, they accused me of endangering the lives of the citizens of Berkeley. Dad was furious. He called and accused them of McCarthyism. I never really was a member of BAMN because I never signed the paperwork in order to become one, so how they got my name I don't know. On Sunday, May 20, 2001 I moved out of the dorm completely and back to 53rd Street.

CHAPTER TWELVE

Graduate School and My 3.55 GPA

I TOOK TWO YEARS OFF BETWEEN COLLEGE AND GRADUATE SCHOOL. In those two years I worked in AmeriCorps, where I tutored elementary and high school students in the Oakland Public Schools. I also slowly began to work on poems that would become my combined fourth and fifth poetry collections, entitled *City Beautiful: Poems 1998–2006*.

In AmeriCorps I worked in an Oakland alternative school called Rock La Fleche. The students who attended Rock La Fleche were prison inmates, students who lived in a group home or students who were simply not doing well in the public school system. The students ranged from grade eight to grade twelve.

The students had three teachers: each taught two subjects. I tutored the students both in the classroom and outside in the hallway. The teachers did not interact with them, except to say, "Here, do this assignment" and then point at the page they had to work on. After that they would sit behind their desks and stick their noses in a book. When the students tried to ask a question they wouldn't answer it. There was one teacher named "Granny" who told the students she would bring a gun to school and called two girls "bitches and ho's." After the end of that year, "Granny" was forced to retire.

I also tutored a fourth grade class at Hoover Elementary School in Oakland. The teacher was only in her late-twenties, about three years older than me. She reminded me of the teachers I had at Park Day and at New Age. She was belligerent. The first day I was there it was Valentine's Day. The kids were full of sugar and were hyper. As she put the video of *Dennis the Menace* into the VHS the teacher said, "In five seconds I want all of you to *shut up!*"

She treated the black boys the worst. She turned the entire class against this one dark-skinned black boy by inviting the kids to make fun of him. Two boys got into a fight in class and she only called the principal on the darker skinned boy. I eventually quit Hoover and went to Rock La Fleche because of the way the teacher disrespected me in front of the class on more than one occasion. One time she told the class, "I don't want to hear your mouth" and then she pointed at me and said, "including yours," like I was one of her fourth grade students. The girls, shocked, asked me, "Are you going to let her talk to you that way?" Looking back I realize that the girls were right. I should have said something to her, and not in a polite way, I might add. Another time she told me to "shut up" in front of the students. That was the day after I had returned from a trip to Philadelphia and New York on an American Airlines flight late at night. That was when I quit.

I wasn't satisfied with AmeriCorps in many ways because of their prejudice towards disabled people and because the ACCORD for Youth supervisors took the side of my bosses and colleagues. I felt that they were saying that I deserved the negative responses I got from people. About a week before the year ended, we all gave oral evaluations. I was surprised that a lot of people had negative experiences with AmeriCorps. I didn't hear what everyone had to say because we were broken up into two groups, but my good friends, two Chinese-American girls, Andrea and Millie, one African-American girl Rashida, and Johanna, a mixture of Nicaraguan and Chinese, all had negative experiences with their bosses and with the two main Corps leaders, Kat and Chandra. They felt that Kat and Chandra also took the sides of their bosses.

I didn't hear what my two colleagues in CASEY Family Programs, Rusty and Megan, had to say because they weren't in my group. I remember another young woman named Maria, who was from Peru originally, had gotten into a fight with the CASEY leader because of her attitude. I wasn't there that day so I didn't hear what the fight was about. I should have taken the cue from Maria that working there was going to have a lot of negative consequences. Maria later transferred to the East Side YMCA in Oakland.

The group leader had a bad attitude towards me. I think it was because she knew I was a published writer. Right before I turned twenty-five, she saw me read at the Black Repertory Group in Berkeley. She was frustrated because I couldn't meet her high standards of how I was supposed to tutor the students. She also didn't take care of her diabetes. On May 2, 2002 we had a staff appreciation evening. The leader was angry at the fact that I didn't work that day at Rock La Fleche. The principal at Rock La Fleche was a Nigerian gentleman. He told me that since there was going to be a staff conference meeting that day, I didn't need to tutor the students. Somehow, something got lost in translation, and she got angry. I don't know how she found out that I wasn't there because I didn't ask.

Anyway, she decided to confront me. She wasn't polite. Mom, Rashida and Millie heard this, even though she had turned her back to them. The leader called me a "disappointment" and a "failure." After that was over, I spilled my food all over the floor, which is something I do when I am angry and nervous. I brought this incident up at the evaluation. Millie didn't seem to remember the incident, but Rashida did. I found out later that the leader hadn't eaten all day, with diabetes, no less. She quit a year later, according to Rusty. I graduated from AmeriCorps on the 19th of July. ACCORD for Youth AmeriCorps doesn't exist anymore.

From July 21–August 11, 2002 I traveled down to New Smyrna Beach, Florida for a three week residency at the Atlantic Center for the Arts. Dad was a Master Artist there and I took his poetry workshop. The other Master Artists in residence at the time were choreographer Doug Elkins and visual artists Janine Antoni and Paul Ramirez Jonas. Mom took Doug Elkins' workshop and she composed two new dances there. One was a solo to "Desperado," a Eagles song from the 1970s sung by fourth through ninth grade Canadian children in The Langley Schools Music Project. They had also sung famous rock-and-roll songs like "Saturday Night." A young talented woman who performed "Desperado" to Mom's score was from Philadelphia.

Doug invited the poets to collaborate with the dancers on works to be shown in a public performance at the end of the residency, so I wrote "Polar Bear," which I performed with my mother, who also created the choreography. Mom and I bought a blue plastic child's wading pool in Daytona Beach for my polar bear character. I "lived" on stage in a wading pool while she moved a polar bear on a big diagonal cross in a repeating pattern inspired by the feeling we had when we studied the bear who inspired the poem one hot day at the San Diego Zoo. At the end of the dance, as the lights came down slowly, Doug sprinkled oatmeal flakes from the perch way up in the flies above the stage, and they floated down like some wished-for snowflakes. Our costume was a pair of gray sweat pants and a gray hooded sweat jacket. Doug called me the "Old Navy polar bear."

POLAR BEAR

He was taken away
from northern Canada,
where he wandered
around his icy territory
in negative twenty-nine degrees
with a wind that made it feel like negative fifty
His tracks remained in the silvery white snow
shimmering with purple tints
in the strong, Arctic sun
"Wooeeeeeeeeooooooh!"
was the sound of the harsh, freezing Artic winds
It stayed this way all year round
In the Arctic he fed himself
ringed seals, snatching them
as they surfaced on
the ice blue colored glaciers
Sometimes he'd surprise humans
They couldn't see him
when he covered his black eyes
to blend in with the snow
Next to the San Diego Zoo
the Arctic was a five star hotel
In San Diego
he wasn't the weight
he was supposed to be
Global warming made it worse
with the shorter winters and longer summers
and the substitute food supply
Bobbing his head
he paced back and forth
on the narrow path
in front of the narrow, concrete swimming pool

the zoo's idea of a natural habitat
It was a hot eighty degrees
at the San Diego Zoo
and felt even hotter confined in the tight space
Everyone stared at him
as he anxiously paced
One, two, three, four, five, turn around!
One, two, three, four, five, turn around!
He wasn't the only one
The Asian sun bear
was doing the same thing up the road
One, two, three, four, five, turn around!
One, two, three, four, five, turn around!
They're usually isolated animals
but the polar bear did have a roommate
who took the situation well
He lay on his back
with his legs up in the air
and a smile on his face
He was in the middle
of a nice, afternoon nap
The day was too hot
for all that white fur
The polar bear jumped into the pool
He gazed up at us, looking very distressed
Splaaaash!
He pushed himself off one wall with one of his huge paws
and flipped-turned over onto his stomach and then back
repeating this routine for a long time
The polar bear was never himself again

He had become a bi-polar bear

The Atlantic Center for the Arts was founded in 1977, the same year I was born. The Associate Artists lived in tiny little apartments scattered around the 169 acres of swampland. Their rooms consisted of just a bedroom and a bathroom. Their weekday meals were in the main dining hall and on Thursdays they would go into town and buy groceries. They put their food in the refrigerator and marked their food with their names for the weekend meal schedule.

The three cottages where the Master Artists lived weren't built until the 1990s and were designed after the homes in Sea Ranch, an unincorporated stretch of Highway 1 in Northern California. (Sea Ranch was built in the 1960s and little did I know that three years later I was going to travel there.) Instead of being built out of redwood like Sea Ranch, the Atlantic Center cottages were built out of pinewood. The cottages consisted of one bedroom, a bathroom, a kitchen and a living room. Doug's cottage had a piano.

My schedule consisted of a bath in the morning, yoga, breakfast, my poetry workshop, lunch, a nap, dance rehearsals, dinner, an event in the evening, another bath since it was so hot and then bedtime. We shared the property with snakes, alligators, an armadillo, a tortoise, birds, insects, spiders, scorpions, raccoons and two feral cats. On the weekends we swam at Canaveral National Seashore.

At the Atlantic Center I met two people who were Associate Artists, my good friends and good poets, Dr. Mursalata Muhammad from Grand Rapids, Michigan, and Dr. Linda Rodridguez-Guglielmoni from Mayaguez, Puerto Rico. Mursalata is an associate professor of English at Grand Rapids Community College. Dad had met Mursalata at Penn State University in State College, Pennsylvania a few years prior to our trip to Florida, where she had been teaching before moving to Michigan. She has two girls ages thirteen and eleven.

Linda is a professor of Caribbean Literature at the University of Mayaguez. Linda was born in San Juan, Puerto Rico, and has lived and studied all over the world in places like England, Michigan, Washington, D.C. and California. Linda is the author of *Metropolitan Fantasies*, a collection of her bilingual poetry among other poetry chapbooks. I saw Linda in June of 2004 when she attended a three week writing residency at the University of San Francisco. I saw her this past October in New York City, where she had traveled for an Atlantic Center reunion. We went to the Metropolitan Museum of Art together.

The Master Artists, Associate Artists and Resident Assistants at the Atlantic Center came from places like Buenos Aires; Freeport; the Bahamas; Honduras; Mayagüez, Puerto Rico; Toronto; Boston; New York; Philadelphia; Baltimore; Washington, D.C; Milwaukee; Grand Rapids,

Michigan; Austin, Texas; Los Angeles and the Bay Area. Mom took the morning dance workshop with Doug Elkins. I liked Doug. Maybe it was because he was hyper, like me. In the afternoon Mom and I practiced the dance routine to my poem "Polar Bear." She was so exhausted that she slept through a very severe thunderstorm one evening. It was incredibly loud. I had never really been in a Southern summer thunderstorm. I didn't hear Mom move or make a sound. Everyone else woke up and that was the talk of the Atlantic Center the next day.

There were other events that soon became the talk of the Atlantic Center. News traveled fast there. One evening four young African-American women, Mursalata included, decided to go into town to read their poetry. A poet in my class named Soul, decided to read her poem about New Smyrna Beach, where she talked about the rednecks who lived in the town. Soul lived in Boston. Ebony, another poet in my class, and the only one who lived in the South and knew how to behave in the South, jumped in the car and turned on the engine just in case she had to flee. That was around sunset. I was with my parents and the other master artists in Orlando attending a fundraising dinner. I heard about the incident the next day during lunch. Lunchtime was the time for gossip.

I wrote up a storm in Florida, producing five poems. "Disney's Cinderella," a modern poem based on the 1950 Disney film, was published in an anthology entitled *Totems to Hip Hop: a Multicultural Anthology of Poetry Across the Americas, 1900–2002*, published by Thunder's Mouth Press in 2003. Almost everyone in the Atlantic Center workshop had a poem published in *Totems to Hip Hop*, along with famous writers such as Peter Blue Cloud, Gwendolyn Brooks, Ana Castillo, Joy Harjo, Jessica Hagedorn, Garrett Hongo, Langston Hughes, Robert Frost, Sylvia Plath, and T.S. Eliot. Many of the poets published in *Totems to Hip Hop* were Dad's former students, family friends and colleagues, including the late Reginald Lockett.

During the first full week we were there, all of the residents made a presentation of their artwork. The visual artists were the most memorable to me. One showed us a piece where we hummed along with an air conditioner. Janine made a sculpture out of six hundred pounds of chocolate. Dad would say, "You could feed the people of Afghanistan" every time he spoke about that piece. Two artists showed us a film in which they traveled through a city visiting laundromats and volunteered to do people's laundry. Dad said, "I didn't know doing the laundry was considered art. Maybe they should wash my clothes."

Dad had a field day with the visual artists' work. For three weeks he made fun of them in class. He would say, "Don't be like that visual artist who hummed along with the air conditioner," and everyone would laugh. After a while Ebony got irritated and I remember her saying, "You need to stop; you need to stop."

One evening Dad got into a heated discussion with Janine and Paul about the six hundred pounds of chocolate that they had shown in their video. Dad told them that they shouldn't waste food because people are starving all over the world. Paul was offended by Dad's criticism, which sparked the argument. I forgot what was said, but there were angry voices and words. Everyone was silent not knowing what to make of the situation. When we got back to the cottage Dad vented by saying that Paul "snapped at him like a rottweiler." Then he barked and growled. Dad said that some conceptual artists were scam artists.

Linda was the mediator between Dad and Janine and Paul. In anger, Linda was told that Dad did not appreciate visual arts. Linda told them that Dad had traveled all over the world to many museums looking at art. Some of his cartoons and drawings have been on exhibit in galleries and have been published. His cartoon predicting that O.J. Simpson would be acquitted and the media's reaction to the verdict was published in the *Amsterdam News*. A year later we saw Janine's art at the Albert Knox Gallery in Buffalo, New York. She was in a picture, lying in a tub. A cow was licking her.

August 10, 2002 was the day of our performance. The performance started at 7:30 PM. The evening opened with a performance of two standard jazz tunes played by Dad on the piano, with Mom on the violin: "I Should Care" and "You Don't Know What Love Is." Doug Elkins, whose improvisations were based on capoeira moves, performed with them. It was my parents' debut as musicians. In 2007 their first CD, *For All We Know* came out. It can be found on cdbaby.com or iTunes.com.

When the audience got in their seats and the lights dimmed, I was first on stage where my poem "Disney's Cinderella" was premiered.

DISNEY'S CINDERELLA

She would wake up every morning
to an evil stepmother and jealous stepsisters
She was treated like a slave, doing the cooking and cleaning
Her stepmother always complained about her food:
"Cinderella, the pasta is too sticky, and the salad has ice burn"
or "Cinderella, the potatoes are a bit too hard"
Then Cinderella was ordered to make their dinner again
One of the stepsisters accused her of stealing
her dark blue boot-cut jeans and white cotton blouse by Guess
The other stepsister accused her of driving her Chevy Cavalier
without asking her when she went to pick up Ivory soap at Duane
Reade
(It turns out that her stepsister's ugly boyfriend had borrowed it)
Her punishment was to go upstairs to her stepmother's room
to hear a long list of new chores
like changing her new baby stepsister's
Pampers Baby Dry disposable diaper,
cleaning the kitchen with Clorox wipes
and wiping down the bathroom with Windex and PineSol
Despite all of this, Cinderella was an upbeat young woman,
she did what she was told, and she was very pleasant
There were times when Cinderella would give up,
like when her animal friends had made
her a dress for the prince's ball
that was superior to Versace and Miyake
and it was ripped apart by her stepsisters
There were other times when she would
lose her temper or her patience
like when her name was called every two seconds
"Cinderella, it's Tuesday night, take out the garbage,"
or "Cinderella, the hamper is full"
She had animals in her corner
like her mice, her dog, horses and birds
as well as her Fairy Godmother
Because of the Fairy Godmother's storied enchantment
Cinderella was able to attend the ball
which was RSVP only
It was held at the Pierre Hotel

and Peter Duchin's band performed
The prince had his eye on her
even though there were hundreds of others in the room
including her stepsisters who had crashed the party
One was eating Krispy Kreme doughnuts even though she was
diabetic
The other was eating a big bag of Cool Ranch Dorito chips
She licked the remainders off of her fingers
The Blue Book crowd was thinking, "How grotesque"
The prince was stunned by Cinderella's beauty
and disappointed that she vanished
all except for her slippers
He arrived at her house in his shiny, gold Lexus
and slipped a glass shoe on her foot, which was more fancy
than the latest shoe by Giuseppe Zanotti
They flew off in his private Lear jet
to honeymoon in Walt Disney World
and Disney's private island in the Bahamas
The angry stepsisters and mother showed up at the gate
but it was too late
Their plane was taxiing out to the runway

The evening came to an end with a piece by the dance class to the song "In My Room" by the Langley Schools Music Project. Doug Elkins choreographed the dance piece and the class sat in chairs using hand gestures and space suggesting the worlds of the song. The Langley Schools Music Project album, *Innocence & Despair*, is on iTunes.com.

After the performance we went to the art gallery. This was the first time I had gone into the art gallery during the entire three weeks that I was there. One young artist wanted me to go to view the art pieces she had made with hush puppies. There were giant red ants crawling all over them. After my red ant incident in Martinique, I stood far away. Linda walked over to the hush puppies and commented, "These must be the hush puppies and look at the red ants crawling all over them."

The next day we flew home. Between the heat, the sweating, not eating that much because of the heat, dancing, swimming and yoga I lost fifteen pounds.

My experiences at the Atlantic Center were really important to how *City Beautiful* really began, but my two years of graduate school at Mills College, a private college in Oakland, was where I wrote most of the poetry that ended up in that volume.

Although Mills is famous for being a women's college, the graduate school is co-ed. I enrolled in the English Department's master of fine arts program, a two-year commitment. First I declared fiction as my focus, because I thought that since I was strong in my sense of writing poetry, it would be good to expand my writing tools, and I was trying to be practical by thinking about earning a living as a young adult fiction writer. The English Department put me on "probation" because they thought my fiction wasn't as strong as my poetry, which made me a little nervous. The word "probation" made me wonder if I had done something wrong. After two semesters splitting my focus between fiction and poetry, I decided to stick with my strengths, and declare a major in poetry, mainly because I felt it had been a long time since I had published a book of poems, and having to churn out about a poem a week was sure to get me enough material to fill a book by the end of two years.

The campus with all its old trees, running creeks, and wild animals (they have croaking frogs, bobcats and mountain lions, skunks and wild turkeys) was also a comfortable place for me. When it was warm out I would sit under the eucalyptus trees, which were all over the place. But I spent most of my time taking classes in Mills Hall, a nineteenth century building that was the first building on campus when Mills opened its doors in 1852. Julia Morgan designed many of the buildings that were added to the campus in the early-twentieth century, including the original library (now the M Center, or Student Center) and her landmark bell tower, famous as one of the first poured concrete structures in the country.

My favorite place was the new outdoor swimming pool at the Trefethen Aquatics Center behind the Haas gym. Actually the pool is ten and a half years old now, but when I was little I used to go to a summer arts camp at Mills where I swam in their old pool near the bookstore, (which is now a patio area adjacent to the commuter's dining hall) so it seemed "new" to me. I like how big it is, how clean they keep the water and the fact that they don't have to use chlorine to do so. And they had a really good coach named Neil Virtue, who helped make my swimming form much more efficient.

During the two-and-one-half-hour poetry workshops that met once a week, I had to hand out my poems to everyone in the class. Then my teacher, Professor Ratcliffe, who liked to surf in Bolinas near his home in his spare time, had someone in the class read my poems out loud, and of course at some point I would read other people's writing. It was nerve-wracking to critique other people's poetry, worrying if I might offend them or stop their creativity if I said something in an awkward way. It took me about a year to learn how to critique other people's writing. And, of course, having to listen to people critique me. Some were so far into the land of denseness in their own work that their opinions did not make any kind of sense to me. Others nitpicked my work to death, attacking inconsistent punctuation and tenses (which I know are weaknesses of mine, but which I eventually get around to correcting by the final draft), and some just didn't know much about writing poetry that sounded like it was written in 2004, instead of sounding like all the stuff we'd read in high school.

Then Professor Ratcliffe would write comments on my pages. Those were very positive, very clear and very helpful. I got "As" in that class. Besides three semesters studying with him, I had an independent course with Professor Elmaz Abinader, which was held in her office. She was also very helpful in her comments. The independent course was her solution to the problem of Professor Ratcliffe going on sabbatical in the spring of 2005 semester. Because of her independent studies class I was able to avoid some of the people from the fall of 2004 poetry workshop who were "out to get me," according to Lateef, who shared the independent studies course with me because he couldn't deal with them either. So not only were Lateef and I able to critique each other's poems, we also got to write a poem in response to a poem that each of us submitted. We really appreciated Professor Abinader for figuring out a positive solution to that situation. I imagine that her accommodation was in part my benefit from choosing a small school, but it was also because Professor Abinader was unusually smart and dedicated about how she worked with people. She is also a wonderful poet, author of *In The Country of My Dreams*.

We used *From Totems to Hip Hop* as our course textbook for the independent study. Professor Abinader wanted us to learn how to analyze poems and get ideas of how to write our poems. My copy of *From Totems to Hip Hop* is scribbled full of my notes on some of the poems.

My thesis was comprised of my poetry. I decided to focus on animals as a theme that connected my poems. I selected animals that have fascinated me for a long time. I researched everything about their behaviors, foods, habitats, histories and temperaments. Some poems were based upon my own experiences—either with live animals of a species, or with dead specimens I had encountered in unusual places. Each poem became a kind of story, especially the ones about camels and llamas, which I have had a thing about since I was a child. The llama poem was based on a dream I had when I was ten years old. The rattlesnake poem was inspired by one rattler, maybe a baby because it didn't have much in the way of rattles—just beginning to show—that slithered across my path in the valley of Bandelier National Monument one extremely hot summer day. When I wrote about raccoons, opossums, deer and squirrels I encountered in my city life, some Mills students expressed surprise that so many animals could be found out of the woods.

I ended up with about fifty poems. To fulfill the thesis formatting requirements, I really had to fuss with my margins, my cover page, and assembling it just right. That was very uncomfortable, but finally I got it in an acceptable form, even in spite of a dying, beloved iBook G4. Professor Ratcliffe was on a sabbatical that semester and I had a fit worrying if he was going to make it to campus in time to sign off on the thesis, which was required if I was going to get my diploma. It makes my stomach upset just thinking about that time again, but everything worked out and now the original copy resides in the Rare Books Room of the Mills College Library.

I published all those poems in *City Beautiful*. Just to show you how writing is never finished, I ended up doing extensive revisions on those poems before they went to press. It took time to get enough distance on what I had written sometimes to see what changes I wanted to make.

In the spring of 2004, I participated in two performances at Mills College. Meredith Monk, who composed "Three Heavens and Hells" to music in 1992, came out to Mills in February to work with the music students on a residency for a few weeks. On Valentine's Day she performed a few of her classic pieces, including "Three Heavens and Hells." After it was performed I got to take a bow. There was one concert in the afternoon and one in the evening. After "Three Heavens and Hells" Meredith Monk performed "The Game: Panda Chant I" and "II" my second favorite song of hers from her album *Meredith Monk: Do You Be*. The music students who participated in the "Panda Chant" were required to wear red and black. I remember one young tall, thin black man with red braids who wore a black suit and red shoes. A young woman with her black hair cut in a pageboy style had on a black dress, red tights and black loafers. At first they all sang and then they stomped their feet in the rhythm of the heartbeat. After that they clapped their hands. There were about fifteen music students on stage with her. You can find both "Panda Chants" on iTunes.

In March of 2004 I also performed with poet Bob Holman. His wife, the late Elizabeth Murray, and Jennifer Bartlett, both painters and Mills alumni, were being honored at the art gallery. My participation in this event was last-minute because during my Tuesday poetry workshop Professor Ratcliffe announced that Holman was coming to the Bay Area to perform and he needed dancers. He asked if we would be willing to participate. The performance was on Friday. There were about ten of us who danced to his poetry. I danced the part of the rose, the sun and the rock. Every time he said one of those words in his poem I had to do a dance. I was wearing a gray velour sweat suit and sneakers. Mom came to the performance with Maha El Said who came from Egypt on a Fulbright Scholarship to study and write about spoken-word poets in the U.S. Professor Abinader and Maha were close friends, so Maha found out about the event through Elmaz.

Graduation day was May 14, 2005. I got my first iPod that day, as a graduation present from my cousin David and his wife Naoko and my Aunt Sonya and Uncle Myron, which made me really happy. I got CDs from David and Naoko and my cousin Greg and his wife Caroline by the artists No Doubt, the Goo Goo Dolls, Bach and Handel. Uncle Michael and Aunt Denise gave me a bouquet of poinsettias. Heather gave me a necklace. I got tons of cards as well. A few days later my iBook G4 was replaced by a more modern model with an Airport card in it.

My friends Heather and Elaine came too. Elaine brought her older grandson, Noah, who was almost six. And of course my parents were there. I ran across the stage, which was the meadow in front of Mills Hall. They had warned the women not to wear spiked heels, because they would sink in the grass, but since I have never in my life worn spiked heels, that was in the category of "not going to happen." The night before, I participated in a poetry reading at the art gallery on campus. I guess I was either really excited or really tired, because I can't even remember what poems I read. After graduation we went out to a late lunch at the Full Moon Restaurant in Oakland.

It was strange to think that my school days might finally be over. I've heard it said that one-fifth of your life is spent at school, but so far I've spent about four-fifths of my life in school. Sometimes now I think about going back to graduate school, maybe to get a doctorate in curriculum planning, because I think that is an area of education where I could really contribute something and it really needs to be rethought, but so far, I have not really done anything serious about looking into that idea. One reason is that I want to get a few more years of experience on me, when I would be closer to the same age of the majority of graduate students. (I was definitely on the young side at Mills, compared to the majority of students.) Another is the problem of paying tuition. I just racked up a big debt to the federal government paying for those two years of graduate school at Mills. But it was worth it; I'd probably do it again.

In college, my grade point average came to something like a 2.89—a B-/C+. At Mills, my grade point average was 3.55—an A. Significantly better, I think, because I was working to my strengths, and able to stay focused on what I wanted to do. Mills was a better fit for me than any of my other college experiences. Maybe it was because I was older, being twenty-six and a half when I started and twenty-eight and a quarter when I left. In college I was eighteen and a half when I entered and twenty-four and a quarter when I graduated. And then, I didn't have to deal with requirements such as Reading and Composition, and Math, or other courses that I struggled with or found absolutely boring, wondering why was I having to do some course that had nothing to do with my major. The classes at Mills were all small seminars, with no more than twelve to fifteen people in a section, and I no longer had to deal with graduate student instructors and discussion sections. The student body was more diverse, and I didn't hear that many ignorant remarks. There were no more than ninety graduate students in the English Department. Having professors that were writers made a big difference. I was also commuting from home and I was eating and sleeping better and exercising more than I did in college. At home I was able to study with no distractions since my room is upstairs and I basically have the upstairs floor to myself.

I still keep in contact with Professor Abinader. I also kept in contact with Jennifer, a young woman who I met in my fall of 2003 Young Adult Fiction course. She is almost seven years older than me. She was thirty-three when I met her. It was nice to have her around because she was older and she had a different perspective on life than I did. She has a husband and two small boys, ages three and seven. She lives in San Francisco. I also have kept in contact with Lateef, who is living on his own now, and Judith, a poet I met in my spring of 2004 poetry workshop. She has one son and two daughters, all around college age now and she is a professor of English at Laney College and the College of Alameda.

CHAPTER THIRTEEN

My Campaign For Oakland School Board, District One

I N MARCH 2008, I HAD TO DECIDE WHETHER I WAS GOING TO WRITE a book about my school experiences as a multiracial, learning disabled, youth, woman—my smorgasbord of identities—and leave it at that, or whether I was going to do something that would assist students in my situation in avoiding the problems I encountered during my years in school. I decided the best contribution I could make would be to seek a seat on the Oakland School Board.

My sister Timothy and my brother-in-law Alex helped me obtain the amount of signatures required to have my name placed on the ballot. Wilson Riles, Jr., a respected African-American leader in Oakland, and a former councilperson and candidate for mayor, and Orlando Johnson also helped me out. On Friday March 7, 2008 I turned in all of the necessary paperwork to the city clerk. We printed cards and posters, bearing my image and stating my position on the issues, which we distributed throughout the district.

I first met one of my opponents, Mrs. Jody London, at City Hall when we engaged in a random drawing to figure out how the order of the names would appear on the ballot. I was asked by the City Clerk to do the drawing. I drew my name first by coincidence. Dad and City Council president Ignacio de La Fuente were in the back laughing about the turn of events that saw me draw my own name.

My two opponents Mrs. Jody London and Mr. Brian Rogers were well known in the North Oakland community. Mrs. London's constant selling point was that she was a parent of a third-grader and a first-grader enrolled at Chabot Elementary School. Chabot School ranked a ten out of a ten when it came to standardized test scores in the District One area. It was also ranked in the top five of schools in the entire Oakland Unified School District. Mrs. London has her own business and has worked with local governments and non-profit organizations. She had a very long list of endorsements. However, her campaign was centered around Chabot School and being a parent.

Our first debate took place at Chabot School before the National Women's Political Caucus-Alameda North, which for some reason omitted my name from the ballot on which the assembled women were to endorse a candidate. They apologized. (The City Clerk's office also failed to list me as among those who had filed. They also apologized. This was an ominous start.) So confined were Mrs. London's interests to the school where her children were enrolled, she wasn't aware that there was a high school in our district, nor did she know the boundaries of District One.

Mr. Rogers is an Oakland native and son of the owner of Dreyers Ice Cream, which was sold to Nescafe for two billion dollars. Though Mr. Rogers is a Republican, Oakland Democrats like City Council President Ignacio de la Fuente, former Governor and Mayor Jerry Brown and Senator Don Perata, leader of the state senate, endorsed him. Given the opposition, I knew from the beginning that my quest for a School Board seat would be an uphill battle, but without my being a candidate there would be no advocate for the left behind, the learning disabled, black and Latino students whose drop out rates are over 50 per cent and who are ill served by schools that lack equipment and resources.

March 31, 2008 was when I began to be interviewed by endorsers such as the Sierra Club, the Green Party, the National Women's Political Caucus-Alameda North, the League of Women Voters, the Hillcrest Elementary School PTA, the Democratic Party, the Rockridge Community Council, the Piedmont Avenue Neighborhood Association and the *Oakland Tribune*. Before I attended the forums, I had to fill out a questionnaire and send it by email to each endorser. I answered each questionnaire as follows. Here are the highlights:

I am running for School Board because I feel that the Oakland School system has failed our children in many ways. I spent the primary grades in the Oakland Public Schools and found unqualified teachers, classrooms that were too crowded and the schools lacked resources that were needed in order for the students to go from grade to grade successfully and to enter college prepared.

In this campaign I am only concerned about my beliefs and I will not conduct a campaign where I will tear up my opponents. The old politics.

My qualifications for office start with being born and raised in Oakland. I attended public and private schools in Oakland. I went to Laney College for two and a half years, which helped me get into U.C. Berkeley. I tutored students in elementary and high schools through AmeriCorps. I then went to Mills College for Graduate School and taught at Merritt College and the College of Alameda. Throughout my writing career, I have traveled to different Oakland public schools and public libraries reading my poetry to students of different ages. I have influenced them to read and write. I'm in a good position to help raise the students' reading scores as someone who initially found reading very difficult. But through hard work, I overcame this obstacle and produced five published books. I also wish to be an advocate for the rights of learning and physically disabled students.

I believe the main issues are:

The standardized tests: When I went to school in the 1980s and 1990s the entire school year was focused on getting ready for what was then called the CTBS tests. I remember being frustrated, bored and extremely nervous because the tests did not cater to my learning style. Basically, I did not understand the tests because they were asked in such a way that I was not able to figure out what was being asked. The tests are difficult for poor students, minority students, students who have English as a second language and students with disabilities.

The textbooks and curriculum: The textbooks are out of date and are biased. For instance, when studying Black History the textbooks discuss slavery and the Civil War. Then they jump one hundred years to the Civil Rights Movement without discussing the Reconstruction era and Jim Crow. The Japanese and Chinese Exclusion Acts, the Philippine and Spanish American Wars, Indian genocide and the annexation of Mexico. The textbooks are written from the point of conservative white historians. In middle school and high school, the students read literature based on lives of the rich white people during the nineteenth and twentieth centuries. This causes frustration and boredom because the students cannot understand the literature because they don't have the life that the characters have.

Qualified teachers: I have written a memoir of my educational life from pre-school through the 2008 Oakland school board campaign. As I flipped through the two hundred or so pages I realized that very few of my teachers were qualified both in public or private schools. When I worked in AmeriCorps in between college and graduate school, I observed the way teachers had treated the students. The teachers ranged in age, race and socioeconomic backgrounds, and were mainly white women. As a student and a tutor, I noticed that the teachers had very nasty attitudes towards the students, particularly the African-American and Latino boys. I noticed that the white students and the female students tended to be treated very differently. One particular school I worked in, which was for students who had failed in the Oakland Public Schools, was one of the worst schools I observed. The students took four courses: Science, History, Math and English. The teachers did not interact with the students. Instead they told the students to do assignments out of the book while they sat behind their desks and read. They didn't go around the room to check on the students. One teacher called the students "bitches" and "ho's" and threatened to bring a gun to school. I think that a major problem is that the teachers are trained to work with one type of intelligence and one type of need. A majority of students do not meet these criteria, which causes nervousness and fear for both the teacher and the student. I also think that competition is not "healthy" or helpful. The idea of competition in the classroom means shaming students in front of their peers if they do not meet the type of criteria I mentioned above. "Healthy Competition" is an oxymoron like "compassionate conservatism."

Overcrowded Classrooms and School Closures: Overcrowded classrooms have been a problem since as long as I can remember. Now with budget cuts this problem has become worse. It is a problem for every student, no matter what race, age, socioeconomic, health or language background the student has. Economic resources are scarce even if the classroom has the right classroom size. If a classroom doesn't have enough desks or chairs for everyone, enough books for everyone, enough paper or pens, etc., the students are going to suffer.

P.E. and Arts: It is unfortunate that P.E. and Arts are not seen as important courses like Math, Reading and Writing are. P.E. is important for children because they need to move around. P.E. was part of my school curriculum and it helped me perform better in the classroom because it calmed me down and it kept me healthy. That is key for students, particularly those with ADHD. P.E., just like eliminating junk food in the cafeteria, is important in getting rid of the epidemic of obesity. Arts like music, drama and visual arts encourage creativity, self-confidence, language and Math skills and help students perform better in the classroom.

Creativity: Children should be encouraged to think for themselves instead of thinking like everyone else. For instance, they should learn that there is not a single way of interpreting a story or poem and that there is not one way to look at a shape or a painting. In order for a student to achieve, parents and teachers should discuss students' progress. Exercise, a healthy diet, music, art, drama, after school programs, summer school and parent involvement are key to a child's learning. Homework help and disabled student resources are also key, and so is bilingual education. Standardized testing does not meet the needs of every child.

Charter Schools: Some Charter schools are necessary like public and private schools. For instance, if a parent wants a child to learn about their culture in a way that a mainstream school environment won't teach them, the parent should be allowed to enroll their child in that type of school environment. Oakland's American Indian High School and American Indian Charter School were rated number one and number two in the entire school district. Even though Native American students make up 0.43 per cent of the population, their test scores only dropped 1 per cent in between the 2005–2006 and 2006–2007 academic years as opposed to white, black, Latino and Asian students whose scores dropped between 7 per cent and 24 per cent. Even the far right *Wall Street Journal* reported that black students did well in African-centric Schools. As an example of the dire situation confronting Oakland Schools, it has been reported that seventeen schools might have to close as a result of declining enrollment. This means that the district will receive even fewer funds from the state.

Credentials: In California, teachers are required to take tests for teaching credentials. They get tested in Math, Reading and Writing, yet they should also be tested in Science, Geography and History. The tests do not guarantee that teachers will be successful in the classroom and they don't train teachers to work with students from different cultural backgrounds, students who have English as a Second Language and disabled students.

Each forum ranged from forty-five minutes to an hour and a half depending on whether the District One candidates were the only ones attending the forum or if the candidates from each district attended. Mrs. London seemed to have home court advantage from the start. The first debate, for example, took place in an upscale, majority white Rockridge district, her turf. It took place at Chabot School, the largely white school that her children attended. I suspect that her emphasis on children attending schools in their neighborhoods appealed to white parents concerned about their children sharing classrooms with blacks and Latinos. Mrs. London's neo-con argument was the latest version of George Wallace's appeal. During the forums and debates she pushed the argument that children should attend schools in their neighborhoods and where their parents own property. In her campaign literature, she presented herself as an advocate of "diversity."

During a question-and-answer period, some of those in the audience at a forum held at the College Avenue First Presbyterian Church, also located in Rockridge, expressed concern about some black students from Claremont Middle School. Claremont Middle School is located down the road from Chabot School. The students were accused of participating in antisocial behavior on their way home from school. Segregated schools means that schools in affluent white districts will receive more funds and support than schools in the "flatlands" where I live. It also means that students will not interact with those who are different from them, which will lead to generation after generation of bigots which, as I have shown in this book, extends to the college level where one hears from students and professors the kind of ignorant rhetoric about unpopular groups that one hears on right-wing talk shows. Mrs. London also received support from Kathy Murphy, the *Oakland Tribune* reporter, who marginalized my candidacy and couldn't resist getting in some digs at Brian Rogers even though he and I lost the race. Even though he was a Republican, Brian Rogers didn't say one thing to white audiences and different thing in his campaign literature. He was also willing to assist African-centric schools like Sankofa and poor schools like Santa Fe.

Even though I didn't succeed in winning a school board seat, I met thousands of people and participated in forums and debates, I got stronger as the campaign progressed. I exchanged views with a mixed crowd. Asian, black, Latino/Chicano and white people spoke to me, as well as rich, middle-class and poor people. Even children asked me questions. I think this was because in my campaign I was advocating on behalf of every child. I stated that the standardized tests did not work for everyone because they did not fit the needs, intelligences, cultures and socioeconomic backgrounds of many of the students. I said that some children learn by movement, creativity and hands-on experience, and that children should be able to go outside of the neighborhood for school if the neighborhood school wasn't a suitable environment for them. I said it was important for students to be around children who were different than them. I was also the only candidate who brought up the importance of a good diet, exercise, creative writing, arts, drama, music and dance. I introduced the idea of using yoga, swimming, basketball and running techniques and better nutrition to release stress, which might be the source of some antisocial activities. I discovered that the situation for blacks and Latinos are worse than what I expected. For example, 70 per cent of the kids who are brought up for disciplinary charges are black. I wasn't surprised to learn from the National Center for Learning Disabilities, founded by the late Carrie Rozele, that 40 per cent of juveniles who appear in Family Court had learning disabilities. A majority, the report found, "had failed in school or had dropped out, and engaged in antisocial and criminal behavior, ranging from robbery to drug dealing to murder."

I was lucky to have advocates who insisted that I receive my rights every step of the way, including my mom, who moved quickly after my diagnosis in my infancy to take steps to provide me with assistance. My dad intervened from time to time when I was getting shafted by teachers and other professionals, and demanded that my rights be respected, if not with his notorious "Ishmael Reed" letters, then by meeting with individuals face to face. These enlightened teachers and counselors understood my situation. Those 40 per cent in juvenile court don't have such a support system.

I use the word "angry" often in my manuscript, which was written over an almost twelve-year period, but now that I look back upon it, being learning disabled wasn't treated as a serious subject as it is now and what came across as anger towards me often masked feelings of frustration, fear and disappointment. My anger towards my teachers came from frustration, fear hurt, disappointment and shame. There seemed to be a cognitive firewall separating me from some of my fellow students and teachers. It was as though I was on an island shouting to people on the mainland, but my pleas were inaudible.

Though denied endorsement by the Oakland political machine which favors incumbency, the Green Party did back me. I welcomed the endorsement of the Green Party. Most of the problems on my street are green-related, such as the shootings and boom cars that put stress on the neighbors and limit their opportunities to exercise. There is a lack of stores that sell fresh, healthy food at an affordable price—what my dad calls "shrines to animal fat and sugar," where the available fruits and vegetables are outnumbered by liquor bottles. Black neighborhoods in Berkeley are located near the freeway causing high rates of asthma. Toxic products like predatory loans, drugs, illegal guns and prostitutes are deliberately aimed at black residents.

The rest of the endorsers turned me down. Maybe it's because Ms. London and Mr. Rogers were older and had more experience than I did on some levels. I was a newcomer. At first, the Green Party turned me down as well, but after listening to me speak to Green Party members who assembled at a fundraising party held at the home of Mr. and Mrs. Lawrence Shoup in Oakland on April 13, 2008, they endorsed me. Their endorsement was not mentioned in the article that *Oakland Tribune* education reporter Kathy Murphy wrote about the School Board race. But the endorsement that excited me the most was the one I received from former congressperson, Cynthia McKinney. Ms. Murphy also failed to mention this endorsement. The daughter of Billy McKinney, a former Georgia State Representative and Leola McKinney, Cynthia has been a fighter ever since a child when she rode on the shoulders of her Dad, who was challenging the racially-discriminatory policies of the Atlanta Police Department. She earned a B.A. in International Relations from the University of Southern California and a Masters of Art in Law and Diplomacy from the Fletcher School of Law and Diplomacy. Her career began when she received 40 per cent of the popular vote and was elected to the Georgia House of Representatives. In 1992, she was elected to the U.S. House of Representatives from the 11th District of Georgia. She was reelected in 1994. McKinney has gained a lot of enemies along the way and Republicans crossing over to vote for her opponents has been seen as the cause of her defeat. Her raising questions about the Bush Administration's response to the 9/11 attacks and Hurricane Katrina have also drawn fire from her enemies. She forced Congress to take a second look at the assassination of Martin Luther King, Jr.

On May 11, 2008 a longtime family friend and non-profit organizer Kim McMillon set up a huge event at Anna's Jazz Island in downtown Berkeley sponsoring myself and Cynthia McKinney, presidential candidate of the Green Party. Anna's Jazz Island owner Anna de Leon sang songs from her CD *The Sweet Bittersweet*. My longtime family friends, Haitian poet Boadiba, poet Karla Brundage, writer Wanda Sabir, former Poet Laureate of San Francisco Devorah Major, poet and my advisor at CCAC Opal Palmer-Adisa, and playwright Cecil Brown read their poetry at this event. As I said before, the late Reginald Lockett was supposed to attend the event but he was very sick. Kim and Dad both emceed the event.

Cynthia McKinney walked into Anna's Jazz Island around 3:00 PM. At first we were concerned about whether or not Cynthia McKinney was going to attend at all. That was because before she came to Oakland she was traveling around to small towns where there was very limited Internet access. She arrived in Oakland at 3:00 AM that morning, still looking fresh. She entered the restaurant about thirty minutes after the program began. She was wearing a bright-pink pants suit and some bright-pink dressy sneakers. Her black hair was wrapped in two French braids. There was a lot of excitement and awe when she entered the room, followed by two filmmakers who recorded our exchange. People whispered to one another and stared at her. Some people took out their cell phones and digital cameras to get photos of her. I shook her hand.

In her speech, Cynthia McKinney talked about how her Dad managed her campaign. She ended up not voting the way he wanted her to vote. She also discussed domestic and international issues. There was a crowd of fifty people at the event. Karla's fifteen-year-old daughter Asha and Karla's best friend Eileen were part of the audience. All three complimented my speech and both Cynthia McKinney and myself got a huge response from the audience with claps, laughter, shouts of "That's right," nodding of the head, and "That was a great speech. I liked it." We both signed autographs. It was great. I was hyped up from that event for several days. I forgot the lack of cooperation from principals who were scared to discuss the bad conditions of their schools, the slights in the media, except for Donald Lacy, moderator of the KPOO debate, who gave me the same respect as he did my older and established rival candidates. Cynthia McKinney inspired me and from her example I learned that in political life, no matter how often you fail you can always rise and succeed. Cynthia is now pursuing a Ph.D. at the University of California at Berkeley.

It was amazing to me how unaware, close-minded and uncooperative some people were throughout the campaign. On Sunday mornings my sister Timothy, my brother-in-law Alex and I would hand out leaflets at the farmer's market on Claremont Avenue in front of the DMV. A lot of the homes around the area had Jody London signs on their lawns. Anyway, I noticed that young people, people of color and middle-aged African-American women were very open-minded. They took my cards and listened to what I had to say. I even ran into Natasha Takara and her little girl, Makayla.

I noticed that a lot of people who walked away or didn't open up their minds and ears to hear what I had to say were upper-class middle-aged and older white woman or older black or white couples. To be fair, some upper-class, middle-aged white women did listen, but most did not. And they were rude about it, too. The most frequent lines I heard were: "I don't want to hear what you have to say," or "I already know who I want to vote for." Then they would say, "Sorry." The three of us would laugh each time this happened and I would say, "Don't say sorry to me because I know you don't mean it." It disturbed me that people would not open their minds. The behaviors of close-minded people are very unattractive behaviors to me. You can say I'm prejudiced towards close-minded people. A lot of them didn't know what district they lived in and didn't know there was a primary election on June 3rd.

Not only were the people shopping at the farmer's market uncooperative, but a majority of the principals were uncooperative. Some of them already had their mind set on whom they were going to vote for. For instance, I met the principal of Peralta Elementary School at the Downtown Berkeley Y. She told me, "We support Jody London." I felt that response was inappropriate. On May 12, 2008 I went to speak with her about issues affecting Oakland schools. When I arrived, she said, "I thought that our meeting was on the 26th." Then she said, "Make it fast."

She told me that the questions that I asked were "inappropriate," which was strange because I had asked people to look over the questions to see whether or not they were inappropriate. "I'm not going to answer any of these questions." Then she told me that she didn't want me to tape-record her. The first question she asked was: "We had a spring festival yesterday at our school. Mrs. London and Mr. Rogers were there. Why weren't you?" I explained to her that I had arranged an event for that date. She shut up. Then she dismissed me from her office. It seemed like a lot of people seemed to rub Jody London's name in my face without thinking about how inappropriate that sounded.

A lot of the principals never replied to my phone calls, including the principal at Santa Fe Elementary School. I would think the principal at Santa Fe would respond because they ranked two out of ten in terms of test scores. It's a majority black school with over fifty per cent of the students' parents receiving Aid to Dependent Children. The principal at Chabot School said he didn't want to meet with me. Instead, he wanted me to send him the questions by email. I did, but he never replied. (It was obvious that he supported Jody London.) The principal at Piedmont Avenue Elementary School, Dr. Hyke, cooperated. Dr. Hyke has a rare type of intelligence for interacting with the students and faculty. Right before I came in, she was with a group of students who were struggling with their reading. I was impressed with how she took time out of her busy schedule to meet with these four first-grade girls. Dr. Hyke had created a diversity outreach program where she brought in students from other cities like Richmond and San Leandro and she also had students from countries like Nigeria, France and Brazil. Dr. Hyke is an advocate for creativity, movement, a good diet and arts in the schools. I saw a classroom of second-graders lined up in the hallway. This class was more racially diverse than many of the other classrooms I visited. During debates I mentioned Piedmont Avenue Elementary School as an example of what each Oakland school should look like.

On May 13, 2008 I did an interview with Kathy Murphy at *The Oakland Tribune*. On Wednesday May 28, 2008 the article was published only giving one paragraph towards my campaign. Due to error, the paragraph that mentioned my platform omitted some words. I wrote a letter of complaint to Ms. Murphy. Here's what I wrote:

"I'm disappointed with the short shrift given to my candidacy for School Board District One by the *Tribune*. Even through I have received an endorsement from the Green Party, a single paragraph was devoted to me and that paragraph seemed to have some language missing. This resulted in a distortion of my views.

"Moreover, even though I gave your reporter my website address, the story lists me as having none.

"I am the only candidate who has questioned the disproportionate appearance of African-American students before disciplinary hearings, about 70 per cent. I have recommended that incentives be given to black and Latino males to enter the teaching professions so that African American and Latino boys will be taught by role models.

"Neither privatization models nor intervention by Sacramento has changed the situation where black and American-born Latino students are reading below proficiency levels. I have fresh ideas about how to change this and how to handle truancy and dropout rates, which constitute a ticking time bomb that will affect the city's future.

"My opponents, both of whom I admire, might have served on more boards and commissions, but I was actually born in Oakland, grew up in Oakland's inner city, and attended schools in Oakland. And so I know the deal.

"Information about my candidacy can be found at www.smartvoter. org. My book about my education *Spell Albuquerque: Memoirs of a 'Difficult' Student* will be published in the fall by CounterPunch press.

— Tennessee Reed"

On May 29, 2008 another article about the School Board race came out, correcting the one that appeared the day before. Here again, the pull quotes in bold type emphasized the candidacy of Jody London and Brian Rogers. I was left out.

After a series of debates, none of which were held in poor or minority neighborhoods, May 31, 2008 was the "final exam" of the School Board race. I went to the Oakland City Hall council chambers. Both the City Council and School Board District One candidates were supposed to attend, but only we three School Board candidates came. We sat in the chairs reserved for council members. KPOO, a San Francisco radio station sponsored the "town hall" event.

The co-host, an African-American high school student, asked very good questions, such as how to bring cultural enrichment programs into the schools and how to address "behavioral problems" in the appropriate manner. I was the only one who could really address being a student who has dealt with punishment as a result of "behavioral problems." Having grown stronger as a debater as the campaign progressed, friends of mine who heard the debate were exhilarated by my performance. An old friend of the family, Jahn Overstreet, son of the famous painter Joe Overstreet, and his mother Elaine heard the broadcast. Jahn said that it was like listening to a prizefight. He said that I won.

June 3, 2008 was the big day. With their money and their army of volunteers, and Ms. London's friends in the media, she placed first. Mr. Rogers placed second. I received nearly 10 per cent of the vote. Hundreds of voters voted for me for me even though I was outspent by thousands of dollars and out-endorsed. I lost, but I put issues affecting poor, disabled, and minority students on the table, something that I know about. In fact, I wrote the book about what is happening to them in school. You just read it. *Spell Albuquerque: Memoirs of a "Difficult" Student.*

Timeline

Assembled by Carla Blank

Indicating some of the landmark events and issues in the history of learning disabilities, special education and testing, particularly within the United States.

1817   The first permanent school in the U.S. for deaf children, the Connecticut Asylum at Hartford for the Instruction of Deaf and Dumb Persons, is founded by Thomas Hopkins Gallaudet and Laurnet Clerc. Gallaudet's son, Edward Miner Gallaudet, will help found Gallaudet University in 1864, the first college expressly for deaf students.

1829   The first school in the U.S. for children with visual disabilities, the New England Asylum for the Blind, opens in Massachusetts. It is now known as the Perkins School for the Blind.

1848   The Massachusetts School for Idiotic and Feebleminded Youth, the first school of its kind in the U.S., is founded in South Boston by physician Samuel G. Howe, husband of Julia Ward Howe, with physician Hervey BaekusWilber, who has been experimenting with educational methods for children with these disabilities in his home.

1852   Massachusetts becomes the first state in the nation to enact a mandatory school attendance law; by 1885, 16 states will have passed compulsory attendance laws, although they are not rigorously enforced. (See: 1918)

1877   German neurologist Adolf Kussamaul coins a term "word blindness" to describe "a complete text blindness…although the power of sight, the intellect and powers of speech are intact."

1881   Throughout the nineteenth century, from as early as 1802, research related to the causes of aphasia, location of speech functions in the brain, and connections between aphasia and speech were being conducted. This year, clinical neuropsychiatrist Carl Wernicke (1848–1905, born in Tarnowitz, Upper Silesia, now Poland) argues that aphasia is caused by problems in connections between auditory and speech areas (motor, conduction, sensory, and total aphasia). His research makes an important contribution to furthering understanding that language consists of two basic functions: comprehension, which is a sensory/perceptual function, and speaking, which is a motor function, and how brain disease or impairment can affect or damage speech and language.

1883   English mathematician and anthropologist Francis Galton (1882–1911), a cousin of Charles Darwin, is credited with coining the term *eugenics* which he defines as the "science of improving stock." This year Galton publishes *Inquiries into Human Faculty and its Development*, where he further states, "Eugenics is the study of the agencies under social control that seek to improve or impair the racial qualities of future generations either physically or mentally." Eugenics theories, integrating the ideas of Darwin (Social Darwinism), Gregor Mendel and Galton, already are influential in the United States. Starting in 1907, legislation will be passed in thirty states to allow sterilization of the mentally handicapped or "feeble-minded." In this same year, Alexander Graham Bell presents a lecture to the National Academy of Sciences titled *Memoir Upon the Formation of a Deaf Variety of the Human Race*, in which he postulates, after investigating the rate of deafness on Martha's Vineyard, that deafness is hereditary. Bell suggests when both a man and woman in a couple are congenitally deaf, they should not marry. (See: 1916)

1887   German physician Rudolf Berlin uses the term "Dyslexia" to describe reading problems where a person has a "very great difficulty in interpreting written or printed symbols."

1894   Maria Montessori (Italy, 1870–1952) becomes the first woman to achieve a medical degree in Italy, and begins working with a psychiatrist specializing in children with learning disabilities at the University of Rome. In 1907, she opens a school in Rome, where she develops innovative sensory-based educational materials and methods. The first Montessori school in the U.S. will open in Tarrytown, New York in 1911. In 1913, Alexander Graham Bell and his wife Mabel will found the Montessori Educational Association at their Washington, D.C. home.

1901   The College Entrance Examination Board gives its first standardized basic aptitude tests, Originally the tests are intended to help level the playing field for students who are not privileged to have received a prep-school education or have parents who attended college. However, because of the way the tests are constructed— with rewards for strategic guessing, a high-speed pace, and cultural biases—over time they come under severe criticism for doing the opposite, as studies show that when admission offices place heavy emphasis on SAT scores, the number of qualified students of color, low-income and women admitted goes down. The tests will become known as the Standard Achievement Test (SAT) in 1947.

1905   Cleveland ophthalmologist Dr. W.E. Bruner publishes the first U.S. report of childhood reading difficulties.

1916   Educational psychologist and Stanford University professor Louis M. Terman (1877–1956) and a team of Stanford graduate students construct an American version of the Binet-Simon Scale, an assessment test to measure individual intelligence, which was devised in 1896, primarily by Parisian psychologist Alfred Binet. Although respected educators and journalists, labor groups and parents charge that racist and class interpretations, rooted in eugenics theories advocated by Terman and other educational psychologists are actually behind the "science" of the testers' conclusions, school districts quickly employ their rating system, known as an *intelligence quotient* or IQ, to academically track students. IQ tests become widely accepted as a standard educational diagnostic tool. Identifying labels, such as "superior and inferior," determine children's educational futures, with "slow" students placed in special classes or entirely separate schools, and the highest-scoring students placed in "gifted and talented" programs with high academic standards. An IQ score of 100 is said to indicate an average intelligence level. Although Terman originally predicts a score of 140 or more indicates "genius or near-genius," later studies argue that an IQ score above 120 reveals little correlation with life work generally considered to have genius. Terman acknowledges that "above the IQ level of 140, adult success is largely determined by such factors as social adjustment, emotional stability, and drive to accomplishment. In other words, an extremely high IQ conveys no practical advantage at all."

1917   The U.S. Army convenes a committee, including Robert Yerks and Louis M. Terman, to develop intelligence tests to screen the intellectual ability of 1.75 million recruits, in order to determine classification into their best service assignment. The Alpha test contains written text for literate recruits and the Beta tests contains pictorial tests for illiterate men and those who fail the Alpha tests, with individual oral tests provided for those who fail the Beta test. These Army tests become the basis for development of future standardized tests, although they do not prove useful in helping determine how recruits will best serve the military effort.

1918   By this year all states have passed a compulsory education requirement.

1921   The American Eugenics Society is founded at the Second International on Eugenics, and becomes a politically and scientifically influential movement for the next few decades. Eugenicists are especially active in Great Britain and Germany, besides the United States, where advocates seek and gain adoption of legislation, which affects public educational reform movements and courses on eugenics, which become common offerings in college curricula. Eugenics theories will again gain influence in public policy debates in the 1990s in the U.S., and continuing to the present, even though eugenics theories are known to have been used to justify Nazi race policies in Germany. (See: 1969, 1994)

1926   The first Scholastic Aptitude Test (SAT) is administered in 353 locations, employing multiple choice questions in its nine test sections of Definitions, Arithmetical Problems, Classification, Artificial Language, Antonyms, Number Series, Analogies, Logical Inference, and Paragraph Reading.   60% of the candidates are male, of whom almost half will apply to Yale University. 27% of the women candidates will apply to Smith College. (See: 1901)

1931   The Department of Special Education is established within the U.S. Office of Education.

1953   The Department of Health, Education and Welfare is established, with Oveta Culp Hobby appointed as its first secretary.

1954   In *Brown v. Board of Education of Topeka* the U. S. Supreme Court redefines the educational landscape when it rules on five cases from different parts of the country that "separate educational facilities are inherently unequal." Although the ruling is passed to remove inequalities between the educational services and opportunities offered to African-American children, as compared to white children, the ruling can also be seen to have implications regarding provision of equal services and opportunities for children with special educational needs.

1963   Samuel A. Kirk (1904–1996) and B. Bateman publish "Diagnosis and Remediation of Learning Disabilities in Exceptional Children," using the term *learning disabilities* for the first time. Kirk uses the term again at a 1963 Chicago education conference on children with perceptual disorders, and the term quickly gains acceptance. The U.S. Department of Education's Office of Special Education and Rehabilitation states that by 1998–1999, about 13 per cent of public school children, ages 0 to 21, or about 6 million students, are identified and enrolled in special education programs. Currently, nearly one-half of all students receiving special education services are identified as having learning disabilities. (See: 1965)

1963   The Association for Children with Learning Disabilities is formed. (It later changes its name to Learning Disabilities Association of America.)

1965   The Division of Handicapped Children and Youth (DHCY) is formed under the U.S. Office of Education (now named U.S. Department of Education). Samuel A. Kirk is appointed the first director by President John Kennedy.

1969   The U.S. Congress passes the Children with Specific Learning Disabilities Act, included in the Education of the Handicapped Act of 1970 (PL 91–230, Title VI, Part G). This is the first federal law, which defines learning disabilities and provides funds to send handicapped children to the public schools, including mandates for support services.

1969   Berkeley psychologist Arthur J. Jensen publishes an article alleging than the average IQ test scores of blacks are about fifteen points lower than those of whites, and that therefore, blacks are, as a group, intellectually inferior to whites. He further argues that because intelligence is an inherited capacity, and races tend to be "inbred," blacks will continue to remain less intelligent than whites. In 1970, William Shockley, a 1956 Nobel Prize winner for physics, advocates a "Sterilization Bonus Plan," based upon this same assessment. Shockley suggests paying "intellectually inferior" people:

> "a bonus rate of $1000 for each point below 100 IQ, [with] $30,000 put in trust for a 70 IQ moron of twenty-child potential, it might return $250,000 to taxpayers in reduced costs of mental retardation care."

When critics charge Shockley's reasoning sounds like Nazi Germany's race policies, he responds: "…the lesson to be learned from Nazi history is the value of free speech, not that eugenics is intolerable."

1970   *Diana v. California State Board* requires that children referred for special education placement be tested in their primary language for a non-biased assessment.

1972   A federal court rules in *Pennsylvania Association for Retarded Children (PARC)* that students with mental retardation are entitled to a free public education.

1972   *Mills v. Board of Education of Washington, D.C.* requires "adequate alternative educational services suited to the child's needs, which many include special education…." It extends the *PARC v. Pennsylvania* ruling of the same year to other students. Similar bills will continue to expand this inclusiveness, regardless of any disability, of the right of all students to a public education.

1975   The U.S. Congress approves Public Law 94–142 (D. 6), the Education for All Handicapped Children Act of 1975, to provide "free appropriate public education" for all handicapped students, ages three to twenty-one. Programs are to be established by 1978, later extended to 1981. The program's special education standards and related services are mandated by the federal government, rather than through state or local government agencies, as is generally the case with educational policies. It includes authorization for federal funding to: make classrooms, physical education facilities and school busses wheelchair accessible; provide 15,000 specialized-education instructors; and to supply assistive technological support, such as computer equipment adapted to facilitate communication for blind and hearing impaired students. Schools must identify, locate and evaluate unique and practical goals and timetables for each student, known as an Individualized Educational Plan (IEP), to determine "whether instructional objectives as being achieved." (See: 1990)

1977   Research institutes on learning disabilities are established with funding from the U.S. Department of Education at Teacher's College of Columbia, the University of Illinois at Chicago, University of Kansas, University of Minnesota, and the University of Virginia.

1983   Public Law 98-199 continues the federal government's pledge to educate handicapped pupils, including preschool through post-secondary-aged students.

1984   U.S. Department of Education's Office of Special Education Programs organizes a task force to consider problems in identification of learning disabilities.

1987   The Interagency Committee of Learning Disabilities issues a report calling for the establishment of Centers for the Study of Learning and Attention, to promote greater understanding of these issues through research.

1990   Congress approves Public Law 101-476, The Individual with Disabilities Education Act (IDEA), a further amendment to Public Law 94-142, which changes terminology from "handicapped" to "disability"; mandates transition services in addition to providing educational services and accommodations. Eligible to children between the ages of 3 and 21 who meet the criteria for one of thirteen qualifying disabilities (autism and traumatic brain injury are added to the previous official eligibility list), and who require special education services because of their disability.

1991   Minnesota passes the first charter school law; in 1992, California will pass the second such law. A "Charter" school can be established with a performance contract that explains the school's mission, goals, programs, assessment methods, and ways to measure success. According to the organization US Charter Schools, charter schools are "nonsectarian public schools of choice that operate with freedom from many of the regulations that apply to traditional public schools. …They are accountable for both academic results and fiscal practices to several groups: the sponsor that grants them, the parents who choose them, and the public that funds them." According to the National Study of Charter Schools Report, "the three reasons most cited to create a charter school are to: Realize an educational vision; Gain autonomy; Serve a special population." They are promoted by politicians, grassroots parent organizations, and private foundations as the newest educational policy, giving opportunities for "parent choice." In 1994, the U.S. Department of Education begins to provide grants to help support charter schools, with $6 million allocated at the start of fiscal year 1995. By 2003, 40 states, the District of Columbia and Puerto Rico will all have approved charter schools, and, by 2007, 4100 charter schools will be serving 1.2 million children.

1994   *The Bell Curve, Intelligence and Class Structure in American Life* by Richard J. Herrnstein, a late Harvard professor, and Charles Murray, an American Enterprise Institute political scientist of Scots-Irish lineage, is published this year and becomes a bestseller. Drawing its title from the normally bell-shaped configura-

tion of the distribution curve that results when IQ test statistics
are graphed, the book argues that mainstream science shows how
intelligence can be used to predict how successfully or poorly
people will function on various sociological and economic indict-
ors such as income level, occupational status, criminal activity,
and unwed pregnancy, and that percentages of achievement or
failure can be interpreted genetically, because of consistent differences between black and white IQ levels. The book is widely
praised in the mass media, including a cover story in *Newsweek*
and interviews aired on major talk shows such as *Prime Time Live*,
Nightline, and *All Things Considered*, and also widely criticized
by many experts, who raise questions about the book's accuracy,
citing flawed or biased and contradictory assumptions and meth-
odology.

1995   All Kinds of Minds, a non-profit organization to train teachers in
       different ways to educate children who are routinely dismissed as
       lazy or dumb when they do not succeed in learning in classrooms
       using standardized methods, is co-founded by pediatrician Dr.
       Melvin D. Levine and financier Charles Schwab, who is dyslexic.
       By 2008, 42,000 teachers will have trained in their methods.

1996   Evolutionary biologist and paleontologist Stephen Jay Gould
       (1941–2002) publishes a revised and expanded edition of his
       1981 book discussing the history of measuring intelligence in
       the twentieth century, *The Mismeasure of Man*, where he refutes
       many claims regarding correlations between race and intelligence
       that appear in *The Bell Curve*. (See: 1994)

1996   California voters pass Proposition 209, known as the Affirmative
       Action Initiative, which "bar[s] all preferential treatment based
       on race or gender in public education and employment in
       California." Although Prop 209 does not affect federally funded
       programs on hiring equity, it does dismantle most state affirma-
       tive action programs in public employment, public education,
       and public contracting. Following California voters' acceptance

of this ballot initiative, many other states adopt similar initiatives. The campaign is underwritten by the Pioneer Fund, which since its founding in 1937 has actively financed controversial research "on race betterment with reference to the people of the United States," besides immigration, and human genetics through educational and other civic institutions. Their mission is to support procreation by descendents of "white persons who settled in the original thirteen colonies prior to the adoption of the constitution and/or from related stocks...."

1997   IDEA reauthorized with new amendments (PL NO. 105-17, 111 Stat. 37). Definition of disabled children is expended to include developmentally-delayed children between 3 and 9 years and ADHD is added as a condition that could qualify a child for services under the category "other health impairment." It includes regular teachers in the IEP assessment process and requires parents to resolve disputes with schools and Local Educational Agencies (LEAS) through mediation.

2002   No Child Left Behind Act (NCLB), a federal bill passed in 2001 to improve teaching and learning standards in the nation's primary and secondary schools by 2014, is implemented this year. All students are to be assessed for their proficiency in reading and math in grades three to eight and once in high school. This includes children in special education programs, although students with disabilities may have the option of one of four accommodations or modifications on their tests, according to legally based criteria, and are to be assessed for "adequate yearly progress." Only children who are home schooled or in private schools are exempt from the testing requirement. The tests are to set high expectations and increase standards of accountability for states, school districts, and schools. Based upon the theories of standards-based education reform, the assumption is that student scores on standardized reading and math tests can indicate a school's educational quality and that sanctions, based on low test scores, will lead "failing" schools to improve their students' education and performance because they will risk increasingly severe penalties if students do not show adequate progress over two or more years. Opponents charge that learning will be compromised because teachers will be motivated to "teach to the tests," and may even cause states or districts to lower achievement goals. Disputes concerning the levels of federal funding levels have continued to grow every year since 2002. As states' education budgets are decreased due to declining tax revenues, and the federal budget's authorized funding for education has continued to be significantly lower than the full amount of funding authorized by the NCLB law, critics charge that more schools will be penalized for failing to meet testing targets, and therefore be denied the resources needed to remedy problems revealed by testing data. (See: 2004, 2008)

2004   To commemorate the second anniversary of No Child Left Behind (NCLB), President Bush announces proposed federal budget increases for Title I funding for disadvantaged students and IDEA in this year when IDEA is reauthorized again, During a speech at West View Elementary School in Knoxville, Tennessee, the President states, "The national objective is to challenge the soft bigotry of low expectations and to raise the standards for every single child." The wording of the new IDEA law is more aligned with the NC LB Act of 2001. Fifteen states are authorized to implement 3-year IEPs on a trial basis when parents continually agree. Concept of "response to intervention," is introduced to increase authority of school personnel and increase procedural safeguards relating to discipline of special education students. However the Fiscal Year 2005 budget proposal, increasing Title I and IDWA by $1 billion each, falls billions short of the funding amount authorized by law, as have all federal budget allocations for NCLB since its implementation. States are left to provide these funds from their own revenues.

2004   According to a Harvard University study, charter school students are more likely to be proficient in reading and math than students in neighboring conventional schools, with the greatest achievement gains reached by African-American, Latino and low-income students.

2004   Joining the trend to use the term "intellectual disability" rather than "mental retardation," the American Association on Mental Retardation (AAMR) is renamed the American Association of Intellectual and Developmental Disabilities (AAIDD).

2007   A report sponsored by Designs for Change, Parents United for Responsible Education (PURE), and the National Center for Fair & Open Testing (FairTest) challenges key strategies of the federal No Child Left Behind law, after test-driven school reforms failed to help Chicago Public School students improve their scores on high-stakes standardized exams. In fact, schools with the most test-based grade retentions proved to have less parent involvement, and test scores that "flat-lined in schools where central office controls replaced local decision making, and top-down interventions over ten years did not work." They recommend following decentralized reforms, which have brought improvements in 150 Chicago elementary schools whose students are "overwhelmingly low income."

2005   U.S. Department of Education releases a report on the high school graduation rates of states, as reported for compliance under the No Child Left Behind law. Presently many states' dropout scores are significantly lower when statistics are interpreted at the state level, as compared to federal calculations. For example, Mississippi's high school graduation rate of 63.3 per cent, as calculated by the federal Department of Education in 2004–05, became 87.0 per cent rate when reported to comply with the No Child Left Behind law. Among the reasons for the discrepancies: no standard tracking system and no national school completion goals were ever set under NCLB; no federal formula to calculate high school graduation rates has been in place until recently; and since higher drop out rates indicate failure—a cause for sanctions—, schools have hesitated to calculate their high school graduation rates using one federal formula, according to an article by Sam Dillon in *The New York Times* (03/20/2008). An article in the *Chronicle of Higher Education* (04/01/2008) states that fewer than 50 per cent of Arizona's students go on to college. At present, Mr. Dillon reports, researchers estimate that nationwide, only about 70 per cent of the one million American students who enter ninth grade each year actually graduate from high school.

2007   Public school systems are serving "600,000 more special education students than [they] did a decade ago, [with] many [students placed] at least part time in regular classrooms," states Benedict Carey in "Calm Down or Else: Unable to handle behavior disorders, many schools use forcible restraint. Is it abuse?" (*New York Times*, 07/15/2008). The article finds that it is common for students to work with staff unaccustomed and untrained to work with severe behavior problems, and that it is not uncommon for schools to respond to behaviors considered inappropriate with extreme measures including having students placed in "seclusion rooms," or removed from the building by police in handcuffs.

2008   The McDonald's Restaurant on University and Shattuck avenues in Berkeley, California, abruptly fires its disabled employees, as reported in "Disabled Criticize Restaurant's Alleged Discrimination Against Employees" (*The Berkeley Daily Planet* (07/31/2008). The article states the McDonald's new owner fired the employees in March, although this new owner avows "I have a strict policy prohibiting any form of discrimination in hiring, termination, or any other aspect of employment."

2008   A coalition of twenty-two disability groups, including the Special Olympics and the American Association for People with Disabilities, calls for a national boycott of the film *Tropic Thunder* after Viacom Inc.'s Paramount Pictures and its DreamWorks unit refuse to remove content from their film which is offensive to individuals with disabilities. The coalition has also requested the studio at least apologize for such content as the character played by Ben Stiller, called Simple Jack, who is repeatedly referred to as a "retard."

Bibliography

Blank, Carla. *Rediscovering America, The Making of Multicultural America, 1900–2000*. NY: Three Rivers Press, 2003.

Kühl, Stefan. *The Nazi Connection, Eugenics, American Racism and German National Socialism*. New York/Oxford: Oxford University Press, 1994.

Online Sources for this Timeline Include:

"10 Myths about the SAT." http://www.fairtest.org/10-myths-about-sat (5/24/2008)

"Children with Disabilities Under No Child Left Behind (NCLB) Myths and Realities March 24, 2004 (updated May 2005) http://www.ndrn.org/issues/edu/NCLB_M&R_Final.htm

Dillan, Sam "States' Data Obscure How Few Finish High School." http://www.nytimes.com/2008/03/20/education/20graduation.html

Important Court Cases in Special Education: http://jan.ucc.nau.edu/~jde7/ese504/class/advanced/courtcases.html www.help4adhd.org/en/education/rights/idea site of the National Resource Center on AD/HD, a program of CHADD

LD OnLine, (a web resource for parents and teachers looking for ways to help students with learning disabilities): "Timeline Learning Disabilities (2006) http://www.ldonline.org/article/11244?theme=print

Lloyd, John Wills. "Chronology of Some Important Events in the History of Learning Disabilities. Curry School of Education, University of Virginia. http://faculty.Vrginia.edu/johnlloyd/edis511/classes/LD_Times.html

McGee, Jennifer. "Bush proposal for No Child Left Behind funding falls short of cities' needs. Nation's Cities Weekly (01/19/04). http://goliath.ecnext.com/coms2/gi_0199-636140/Bush-proposal-for-No-Child.html

"New Report Challenges Strategies Promoted by Chicago School Officials and 'No Child Left Behind.'" (01/18/2007) http://www.fairtest.org/new-report-challenges-strategies-promoted-chicago-0

"No Child Left Behind" After Six Years: An Escalating Track Record of Failure: http://www.fairtest.org/NCLB-After-Six-Years (5/24/2008)

Sass, Edmund, Ed.D.. Professor of Education. College of Saint Benedict/St. John's University. American Educational History: A Hypertext Timeline. http://cloudnet.com/~edrbsass/educationalhistorytimeline.html

Stoskepf, Alan. "The Forgotten History of Eugenics," Vol. 13 No. 3, Rethinking Schools Online. http://www.rethinkingschools.org/archive/13_03/eugenic.html

Students with Disabilities (U.S. Department of Education, Office of Special Education and Rehabilitation's chart of Percentage of all students served by federally supported programs for students with disabilities.) www.inforplease.com/ipa/A0779380.html

"US Charter Schools," history and overview. http://uscharterschools.org

Wikipedia: The Free Encyclopedia. Wikimedia Foundation Inc. Entries include: http://en.wikipedia.org/wiki/ Eugenics (Retrieved 5/24/2008); http://en.wikipedia.org/wiki/ Individuals with Disabilities Education Act (Retrieved 5/24/2008); http://en.wikipedia.org/wiki/ No Child Left Behind (Retrieved 5/25/2008); http://en.wikipedia.org/wiki/ The Bell Curve (Retrieved 5/26/2008)

AK Press

Ordering Information

AK Press
674-A 23rd Street
Oakland, CA 94612-1163
U.S.A
(510) 208-1700
www.akpress.org
akpress@akpress.org

AK Press
PO Box 12766
Edinburgh, EH8 9YE
Scotland
(0131) 555-5165
www.akuk.com
ak@akedin.demon.uk

The addresses above would be delighted to provide you with the latest complete AK catalog, featuring several thousand books, pamphlets, zines, audio products, video products, and stylish apparel published & distributed by AK Press. Alternatively, check out our websites for the complete catalog, latest news and updates, events, and secure ordering.

Also Available from AK Press

The first audio collection from Alexander Cockburn on compact disc.

Beating the Devil

Alexander Cockburn, ISBN 13: 9781902593494 • CD • $14.98

In this collection of recent talks, maverick commentator Alexander Cockburn defiles subjects ranging from Colombia to the American presidency to the Missile Defense System. Whether he's skewering the fallacies of the war on drugs or illuminating the dark crevices of secret government, his erudite and extemporaneous style warms the hearts of even the stodgiest cynics of the left.

Available from CounterPunch/AK Press

Call 1-800-840-3683 or order online from
www.counterpunch.org or www.akpress.org

The Case Against Israel
by Michael Neumann

Wielding a buzzsaw of logic, Professor Neumann dismantles plank-by-plank the Zionist rationale for Israel as religious state entitled to trample upon the basic human rights of non-Jews. Along the way, Neumann also offers a passionate amicus brief for the plight of the Palestinian people.

Other Lands Have Dreams: From Baghdad to Pekin Prison
by Kathy Kelly

At a moment when so many despairing peace activists have thrown in the towel, Kathy Kelly, a witness to some of history's worst crimes, never relinquishes hope. *Other Lands Have Dreams* is literary testimony of the highest order, vividly recording the secret casualties of our era, from the hundreds of thousands of Iraqi children inhumanely denied basic medical care, clean water and food by the US overlords to young mothers sealed inside the sterile dungeons of American prisons in the name of the merciless war on drugs.

Dime's Worth of Difference: Beyond the Lesser of Two Evils
Edited by Alexander Cockburn and Jeffrey St. Clair

Everything you wanted to know about one-party rule in America.

Whiteout: the CIA, Drugs and the Press
by Alexander Cockburn and Jeffrey St. Clair, Verso.

The involvement of the CIA with drug traffickers is a story that has slouched into the limelight every decade or so since the creation of the Agency. In *Whiteout*, here at last is the full saga.

Been Brown So Long It Looked Like Green to Me: the Politics of Nature
by Jeffrey St. Clair, Common Courage Press.

Covering everything from toxics to electric power plays, St. Clair draws a savage profile of how money and power determine the state of our environment, gives a vivid account of where the environment stands today and what to do about it.

Imperial Crusades: Iraq, Afghanistan and Yugoslavia
by Alexander Cockburn and Jeffrey St. Clair, Verso.

A chronicle of the lies that are now returning each and every day to haunt the deceivers in Washington and London, the secret agendas and the underreported carnage of these wars. We were right and they were wrong, and this book proves the case. Never leave home without it.

Why We Publish CounterPunch

By Alexander Cockburn and Jeffrey St. Clair

TEN YEARS AGO WE FELT UNHAPPY ABOUT THE STATE OF RADICAL JOURN-alism. It didn't have much edge. It didn't have many facts. It was politically timid. It was dull. CounterPunch was founded. We wanted it to be the best muckraking newsletter in the country. We wanted it to take aim at the consensus of received wisdom about what can and cannot be reported. We wanted to give our readers a political roadmap they could trust.

A decade later we stand firm on these same beliefs and hopes. We think we've restored honor to muckraking journalism in the tradition of our favorite radical pamphleteers: Edward Abbey, Peter Maurin and Ammon Hennacy, Appeal to Reason, Jacques René Hébert, Tom Paine and John Lilburne.

Every two weeks CounterPunch gives you jaw-dropping exposés on: Congress and lobbyists; the environment; labor; the National Security State.

"CounterPunch kicks through the floorboards of lies and gets to the foundation of what is really going on in this country", says Michael Ratner, attorney at

YOU CANNOT MISS ANOTHER ISSUE

Name _____

Address _____

City _____ State _____ Zip _____

Email _____ Phone _____

Credit Card # _____

Exp. Date _____ Signature _____

- ☐ 1 year **$45**   ☐ 2 year **$80**   ☐ Donation Any Amount
- ☐ 1 year email **$35**   ☐ 2 year email **$65**   ☐ Low-income/student/senior **$35**
- ☐ 1 year both **$50**   ☐ 2 year both **$90**   ☐ Low-income/student/senior email **$30**

A one year subscription consists of 22 issues. The email version is a PDF emailed to the email address you include. Please notify CounterPunch of email and mailing address changes. Low-income/student/senior subscriptions are 1 year only.

Send Check/Money Order to: **CounterPunch, P.O. Box 228, Petrolia, CA 95558**
Canada add $12.50 per year postage. Others outside US add $17.50 per year.
Visit our website for more information: **www.counterpunch.org**

The Secret Language of the Crossroads
How the Irish Invented Slang

By Daniel Cassidy

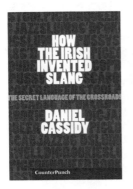

In *How the Irish Invented Slang: The Secret Language of the Crossroad*, Daniel Cassidy co-director and founder of the Irish Studies Program at New College of California cuts through two hundred years worth of Anglo academic "baloney" and reveals the massive, hidden influence of the Irish language on the American language.

Irish words and phrases are scattered all across the American language, regional and class dialects, colloquialism, slang, and specialized jargons like gambling, in the same way Irish-Americans have been scattered across the crossroads of North America for five hundred years.

In a series of essays, including: "Decoding the Gangs of New York," "How the Irish Invented Poker and American Gambling Slang," "The Sanas (Etymology) of Jazz," "Boliver of Brooklyn," and in a *First Dictionary of Irish-American Vernacular*, Cassidy provides the hidden histories and etymologies of hundreds of so-called slang words that have defined the American language and culture like *dude, sucker, swell, poker, faro, cop, scab, fink, moolah, fluke, knack, ballyhoo, baloney*, as well as the hottest word of the 20th century, *jazz.*